Skin

First published in 2009 by
Zest Books, an imprint of Orange Avenue Publishing
35 Stillman Street, Suite 121, San Francisco, CA 94107
www.zestbooks.net

Created and produced by Zest Books, San Francisco, CA

Typeset in MrsEaves

Teen Nonfiction / Health / Beauty

Library of Congress Control Number: 2009933016
ISBN-13:978-0-9800732-5-6
ISBN-10:0-9800732-5-1

CREDITS
EDITORIAL DIRECTOR/BOOK EDITOR: Karen Macklin
CREATIVE DIRECTOR: Hallie Warshaw
ART DIRECTOR/GRAPHIC DESIGNER: Tanya Napier
WRITER: Lori Bergamotto
ILLUSTRATOR: Kunkamon Taweenuch
ADDITIONAL RESEARCH: Nikki Roddy
PRODUCTION DESIGNER: Steve Caramia
MANAGING EDITOR: Pam McElroy
TEEN ADVISORY BOARD:
Atticus Graven, Lisa Macklin, Andrea Mufarreh, Trevor Nibbi, Sasha Schmitz

Printed in China
First printing, 2009
10 9 8 7 6 5 4 3 2 1

Every effort has been made to ensure that the information presented is accurate. Readers are strongly advised to read product labels, follow manufacturers' instructions, and heed warnings. The publisher disclaims any liability for injuries, losses, untoward results, or any other damages that may result from the use of the information in this book.

Medical Advisor: Rachel Herschenfeld, MD
Author photograph by Dan Hallman

Langone Medical Center

Lori Bergamotto will donate 20% of her author proceeds to the NYU Langone Medical Center's Interdisciplinary Melanoma Cooperative Group (IMCG). The IMCG is a multi-investigator research program aimed at advancing prevention, earlier detection, and improved treatment of melanoma through active collaborations between scientists and clinicians.

Skin
THE BARE FACTS

Lori Bergamotto

CONTENTS

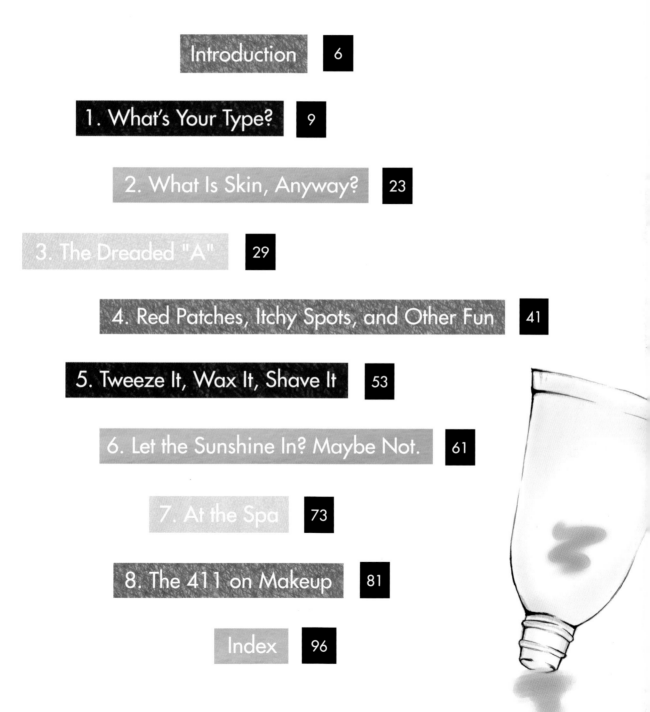

In the story of your life, your skin plays a starring role.

It's the part of you that is most exposed to the world, so it sees everything—windy weather, ski trips, beach days, swim meets, sweaty workouts. It also *shows* everything, from dirt and stress to sunburns, wrinkles, dimples, and—of course—acne. And when you don't feel good about your skin, it can be hard to feel good about yourself. But taking care of your skin can be easy once you know what makes it tick.

In this book, you'll learn about good skin practices to adopt and bad habits to avoid. Also included are scientific explanations for zits and other skin problems, advice on skin cancer prevention, the lowdown on hair removal, tips and tricks for using makeup, and fun recipes for at-home facials. Whether your skin is light or dark, dry or oily, sensitive or acne prone, this book will give you the information and advice you need to make the most of it.

I once struggled with acne myself, so I know what it's like to deal with skin issues (and avoid mirrors at all costs!). But, armed with some knowledge, a helpful dermatologist, and a healthy approach to my, ahem, bumpy situation, I got through it unscathed and (remarkably) unscarred. Years later, I became a beauty writer for magazines and a television beauty and style correspondent, and I have since become passionate about the subject of skin. To write this book, I interviewed medical doctors, acupuncturists, reflexologists, aestheticians, nutritionists, makeup artists, and real teenagers like you. My hope is that this guide helps you learn the ins and outs of skin care so you can keep yours healthy and looking beautiful.

And always remember that no matter how much acne you have, how red your skin gets, or how badly you wish you weren't looking greasy by lunchtime, none of that compromises who you are on the inside. Skin—like everything else in life—has its good days (and years) and its bad. So, if you're having a hard time with yours, remember that it will likely change, and that you can tip the balance in your favor if you start taking care of it now.

Lori

Bergamotto

CHAPTER 1

What's Your Type?

You know what type of person you are and the kinds of things that make you happy, irritate you, and totally piss you off. In the same way, it's important to know what type of skin you have. Of course, just like your personality, it's not always cut and dry. Your skin might be a combination of things—oily, dry, sensitive—but if you know your general skin type, you're on the way to knowing how to make it happy. Take this quiz to figure out your type, then learn how you can start making the most of your skin.

1. At 11 am on a typical school day you find yourself desperately searching for:

A Your cell phone, a granola bar, your lipstick...nothing that has to do with skin care.

B Blotting paper or anything that will help sop up the shine from your face.

C A moisturizer major enough to treat your face, which feels like stone.

D Concealer to tone down the Elmo-like redness on your cheeks, or any kind of calming cream to soothe your raw-to-the-touch skin.

E Any or all of the above, depending on the day, the season, your mood, or what you ate for breakfast.

2. When you touch the skin on your face it feels:

A Just fine, thanks.

B Slick (and not in a cool way).

C Tight and stiff, and—oh, look!—lots of white stuff peels off, too.

D Tender and sore to the touch. Ouch.

E Depending on the day, it's either oil-slick smooth or flaky and scaly.

3. On average, you break out:

A Once in a while, maybe when you get your period.

B All. The. Time.

C Occasionally, but way more frequently in the winter or colder weather.

D Often, but especially when you use a new product.

E Frequently, but only in the same spots on your face.

4. After you shower, your face feels:

A Squeaky clean—and that's about it.

B Momentarily immaculate—but you know a greasy film is on its way.

C Somewhat stiff and dehydrated.

D Scrubbed and stripped—like your face is bare.

E Tight in some places, but OK everywhere else.

5. Your biggest makeup complaint is:

A None really, except that you wish you had more of it.

B It seems to slide right off your face.

C Your lip gloss makes your already chapped lips even drier.

D Everything you test out seems to upset your skin.

E If it's not fading in some spots after an hour, it's highlighting dry patches in others.

KEY:

MOSTLY A'S: NORMAL

You should be fired up to have this rare skin type. Basically when you try out a new product, your skin doesn't flinch a bit: No rashes, blemishes, or sudden dryness can victimize your skin of steel. And whether or not you're over that breakup from last year, your skin is about as resilient as it gets. For you, neither blemishes nor an uneven complexion are frequent, and when they do make an appearance it's usually due to hormonal fluctuations caused by your period or brought on by stress.

MOSTLY B'S: OILY

OK, full disclosure: Yes, this is the type that's most acne prone. But—and pay attention before you panic—oily skin is treatable and, in the long run, may wrinkle less as you age. (That may seem like small consolation now, but you'll appreciate it later—just ask your mom.) If you have this type of skin, you are likely to have large pores, particularly on the nose and forehead, and are tasked daily with trying to sop up the shine on your face. In addition to genetics (thanks Mom and Dad), you can credit an overactive sebaceous gland (the gland that produces sebum, a fatty kind of oil) for your shiny complexion.

MOSTLY C'S: DRY

You haven't been to the beach in months, but your skin feels parched and is peeling constantly. Or, maybe it just feels tight and a little stiffer than is comfortable. Here's why: Your skin cells can't hold on to water as efficiently as they should. Now, maybe it's only once in a while that you experience intense, so-dry-it-hurts skin dehydration after being in an overheated room for a while. Or maybe, even after you drown yourself in moisturizing cream, your skin still feels parched. Either way, it still counts as dry skin.

MOSTLY D'S: SENSITIVE

You might have survived your last breakup, but your skin isn't so tough. It has an abnormally acute reaction to even those products that claim to be "gentle." This skin usually reacts to fragrances and preservatives, and acts out by swelling or turning red or getting bumpy. You might be prone to other allergies as well, experiencing reactions from such things as wool, certain dog breeds, and beauty products that aren't hypoallergenic.

MOSTLY E'S: COMBINATION

Feeling like your skin is a little schizophrenic? Some days it's a little dry on your cheeks, other times it's a bit oily in your T-zone (forehead-nose-chin area), or vice-versa. So what's the deal? You have combination skin, friend, and it's actually more common than you think. It's a little bit dry, a little bit oily, and a whole lot unpredictable.

FINDING THE Rx FOR YOUR SKIN

So now that you know what your skin type is, the second half of the equation is figuring out how to keep it healthy and beautiful. That doesn't mean it will ever be absolutely perfect. No one—not even those supermodels you see splashed across the pages of your favorite magazine—has perfect skin. Or perfect anything for that matter. (They just have professional makeup artists and retouchers.) But with a little knowledge and effort, most people can keep their skin looking and feeling healthy. You and your skin are going to live with each other for a long time, so it's important that you learn how to get along.

On the following pages you will find some suggestions for the four common skin types. If you have combination skin, you'll want to read both the oily and dry categories and see which recommendations work best for you. And even if the quiz showed you to be predominantly one skin type, read about how to treat all of them, as many of us have bits of each kind.

Normal Skin

The scoop: When it comes to this type, think: If it ain't broke don't fix it. In other words, don't use a whole lot of unnecessary products just because they smell pretty or come in fancy packages or because some advertisement swears that you *need* it. Keep it simple.

Your daily cleansing ritual: Try to stick to a routine of cleansing with a mild soap and following up with a lightweight moisturizer that contains antioxidant ingredients such as pomegranate or green tea.

Products and practices to use: Exfoliate with a mild scrub every week or two, particularly if you live in a climate that has drastic seasonal shifts, if you play a sport that makes you sweat a lot, or if you spend a lot of time outdoors.

Products and practices to avoid: Refrain from OD'ing on beauty products. Just because your skin can withstand a lot of different ingredients doesn't mean you should tempt fate by using everything.

Oily Skin

The scoop: Your biggest battles are against blackheads, pimples, and a shiny complexion—and because your scalp is probably also oily, it may be hard to skip a shampoo without feeling like a grease ball.

Your daily cleansing ritual: To prevent and treat breakouts, which oily skin is prone to experience, try foam cleansers and moisturizers that contain salicylic acid.

Products and practices to use: Because your sebum production is working double-time, dermatologists agree that exfoliation is key for keeping extra oil from clogging up pores, which can swell into dreaded blackheads. As for that slick scalp, look for shampoos that contain coal tar ingredients to get more mileage out of your wash-and-wear 'do.

Products and practices to avoid: Though it can be hard to stay diligent about washing your face every single night before bed (or after any kind of sweat-producing activity), you have to be committed to doing so. The last thing oily skin needs is more bacteria introduced into the fray. Avoid any products that promise intense hydration (your skin needs moisture, yes, but it does not need the same amped-up kind of hydration as dry skin). And, if you can, try to stay away from anything that doesn't say it's oil-free.

Dry Skin

The scoop: Your skin is dehydrated and needs extra moisture. Sometimes a seasonal change or an environmental reason (hello, stuffy indoor heaters) is the culprit for your parched skin.

Your daily cleansing ritual: Look for a gentle cleanser with non-detergent-based ingredients like corn or sugar, as opposed to sodium lauryth sulfate, which can strip away your skin's last bit of oil. You can also try skin care products with ingredients like ceramides and fatty acids. These are miracle workers for sealing in moisture.

Products and practices to use: If your dry skin flares up in a red patch, you can try ceramides, which are found in many moisturizers. You can also try to calm down your skin with products that contain calendula or chamomile extract, both known for their anti-inflammatory properties. Also, use products that contain antioxidants, which are especially good for dry skin because they can block free radicals (little molecules that cause wrinkles, which dry skin is especially susceptible to) and balance out your characteristically uneven complexion. Look for antioxidant ingredients like polyphenols or green tea extract.

Products and practices to avoid: Keep away from foaming formulas; those can potentially dissolve lipids (the fats in your skin), and those fats are essential to dry skin because they provide moisture. Also, use a light touch with exfoliation. Your skin simply can't handle being manhandled. If you can't keep yourself from scrubbing your face within an inch of its life, try switching to your less dominant hand while sloughing off that peeling skin.

Sensitive Skin

The scoop: Sensitive skin is more prone to things like redness, small bumps, and itchy patches of uneven skin tone, as opposed to blackheads or whiteheads. If your skin is sensitive, then it's particularly fussy, in which case you need to use the gentlest, least abrasive products that will soothe it and, most of all, not send it into a tizzy.

Your daily cleansing ritual: The same ceramides and fatty acids that you'd use to lock in moisture on dry skin are also recommended for sensitive skin because they help bolster your skin's barrier repair function—essentially your skin's line of defense. Hypoallergenic ingredients, which are those that cause fewer allergic reactions, are also key for your type. (See more about hypoallergenic products on page 90.) If you're truly allergic to many things, you should also avoid fragrances. If you want to use natural products, look for something that contains an ingredient like olive oil. It's a good option for a cleanser because it's unlikely to cause an allergic reaction and it will provide a healthy boost of moisture.

Products and practices to use: To soothe your skin, use topical ingredients like fever few, aloe vera, chamomile, and green tea, all of which are anti-inflammatories that your delicate skin can handle.

Products and practices to avoid: You want to steer clear of anything that can cause your skin to freak out, so if you find products that work for you, stick with them. Be wary of perfumed laundry detergents, scented lotions, and fabrics other than cotton; try new things one at a time, so if you get a reaction you know what's causing the problem. Even gold jewelry can make you get red bumps if your skin doesn't like it. (Not cute.)

sunscreen is good for all skin types

No matter your skin type, it's smart to get in the habit of putting on sunscreen *every* day—especially if you live in a sunny place or spend a fair amount of time outdoors. Sunscreen, with an SPF (sun protection factor) of at least 30, will help prevent sun damage that could later lead to skin cancer, as well as stave off wrinkles. When choosing a daily facial sunscreen, take these factors into account.

Normal skin: Use a regular broad-spectrum sunscreen of SPF 30.

Oily skin: Opt for something oil-free, so as to prevent pimples.

Dry skin: Use a lotion formula with extra moisturizers, as well as antioxidants to further help prevent wrinkles.

Sensitive skin: Choose physical blockers, like zinc oxide, rather than chemical blockers (i.e. Avobenzone), which could potentially set off your skin. (See page 70 in Chapter 6 for more on the difference between physical and chemical blockers in sunscreen.)

And turn to Chapter 6 on page 61 to learn more about the effects of the sun on your skin.

Cleanser, toner, and moisturizer, Oh my!

The shelves are jam-packed with products galore, but which ones do you really need? And what—exactly—do they do?

CLEANSER

What it is: A facial soap used to remove dirt, grime, and bacteria from your skin.

Do you need it? Yes. Use it in the morning, at night, and as needed (post-workout, for example). If you are acne-prone, dermatologists suggest choosing one that contains salicylic or glycolic acid to help prevent acne. Some cleansers also act as a gentle daily exfoliant.

SCRUB

What it is: A gel-like or liquid substance, usually made with either sugar or salt granules, used to slough off dead skin.

Do you need it? Your skin will do this shedding process on its own, but not as efficiently. If you find that your skin is looking dull or that you have uneven flaky patches, you might be due for a little polish. For normal skin, try a scrub once a week. If your skin is dry or oily, opt for about twice a week. If you have sensitive skin, proceed with caution: Find the gentlest exfoliant out there and use it only a few times a month.

MOISTURIZER

What it is: A creamy substance that hydrates skin and keeps it soft and supple.

Do you need it? Yes, and every day. It seems obvious if you have dry skin to use a moisturizer, but even if you have oily or sensitive skin, moisturizer will help your skin stay balanced. Plus, frequent moisturizing with the right formulas can help reduce the appearance of fine lines as you age.

TONER

What it is: An antiseptic astringent formulated to remove dirt and oil as an extra step to cleansing.

Do you need it? It's up to you. If you're really oily and feel like it helps you, use it. If you're very dry and it makes your skin feel tight or uncomfortable, skip it.

Sure, there are lots of products you can use to improve your skin, but the fruits and veggies you eat can also affect your complexion. Here are five superfoods that contain some of the best good-for-your-skin ingredients. Eat these foods regularly, and look for them in natural skin care products.

TOMATOES

Day Job

A salad staple and pasta partner-in-crime.

Secret Agent

Lycopene. In addition to reducing cancer risk and heart disease, lycopene, the natural pigment that makes tomatoes red, is one of the most powerful antioxidants and will help fight off free radicals (see page 15) and keep your skin looking smooth and healthy.

BLUEBERRIES

Day Job

Yogurt topping or breakfast muffin ingredient.

Secret Agent

Chock-full of amino acids, vitamins, and antioxidants, this berry can help stave off wrinkles and prevent certain types of cancer.

miracle produce

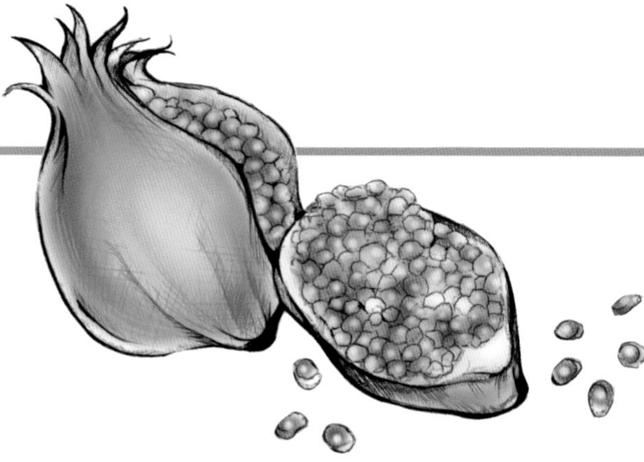

POMEGRANATES

Day Job

Complicated-to-eat fruit that is transformed into a trendy, dark-and-delicious tart juice.

Secret Agent

A powerhouse of an antioxidant, this extract not only helps fight wrinkles but also helps calm inflammation and prevent skin cancer.

ACAI [Ah-Sigh-EE]

Day Job

Brazilian fruit found in breakfast bowls and yummy organic smoothies.

Secret Agent

Packing a major antioxidant punch, this berry can help keep skin looking young and skin tone even.

SPINACH

Day Job

Green, leafy vegetable stongly disliked by children and loved by Popeye.

Secret Agent

A vital source of vitamins A, C, and E—not to mention caretonoids—spinach can also be key in preventing skin cancer.

HEALTHY SKIN PRACTICES

Now that you know what works for your particular skin type, here are some tips that work for everyone's complexion.

Stop Smoking (or better yet, don't start!)

Everyone knows smoking is terrible for your heart and lungs, but it also has a dull, drying effect on your complexion and will speed up the aging process around your lips, giving you dreaded morgue mouth.

Drink Water

Many experts agree that drinking water is good for your skin (not to mention for your body) because it keeps you hydrated and flushes toxins out of the system. And considering that an average 60 percent of your body weight is made up of water, it's easy to see why keeping your system happily hydrated is important. Up your water intake and see if it works for you.

Eat Fish

Many nutritionists swear by the miracle powers of salmon, which is rich in omega-3 fatty acids—a good fat that is high in antioxidants. They claim that eating salmon a couple of times a week can add radiance to your complexion and softness to your skin.

Protect Your Skin From the Sun

Unprotected sun exposure can kick the aging process into high gear, and it can put you at risk for skin cancer (read Chapter 6 to learn more). Use sunscreen!

Exercise

Getting your heart pumping can give you healthier, more balanced skin. Exercise calms the stress hormones that trigger acne breakouts; it also helps increase circulation, which allows zit-inducing toxins to be flushed from the body.

Sleep More

Studies have shown that getting 8 to 10 hours of sleep a night could lead to a more even complexion. While you snooze, the hormone melatonin is produced, and experts believe that it works like an antioxidant, thus benefiting the skin.

QUESTIONS and Answers

Can your skin type change over the course of your life?

A: Definitely. Hormones—which play a large role in the appearance of your skin—and environmental factors can alter your skin as you age. Women who had oily skin growing up may find it drier after menopause (way down the line). The best thing you can do for your skin as you age is to pay attention to it and act accordingly. If you notice that your once tough-as-nails skin is becoming sensitive, take note of what—if anything—you've been doing differently. If your onetime oily complexion becomes parched, bulk up on a moisturizer and consider adding a serum into your routine. Your skin—like the rest of you—will evolve over time, but it doesn't have to be scary and you don't have to be unprepared.

What determines your skin type?

A: While genetics determines your natural skin type, there are other factors that contribute to what kind of skin you will have throughout your life, like the climate you live in and your diet. Stress can even contribute to how your skin behaves, causing it to be extra sensitive during certain periods of your life.

CHAPTER 2

What is Skin, Anyway?

So, now you know your skin type. But what exactly is your skin made of, and what does it do?

Skin is the largest organ in your body. It covers your frame to protect your bones, organs, and muscles from injury and UV radiation. It also houses sweat glands that help to regulate your body temperature, is the barrier that prevents toxic chemicals from entering your bloodstream, and stops water from seeping into your body when you swim or bathe. Skin even helps to produce vitamin D, which regulates calcium levels in the body, and might even protect against certain cancers.

Though people use the expression "skin-deep" to mean that something is shallow, skin actually has a lot of depth. It's composed of three layers: the epidermis, the dermis, and subcutaneous tissue. Check out the diagram below for a visual, and see the following pages for a rundown of what each layer does.

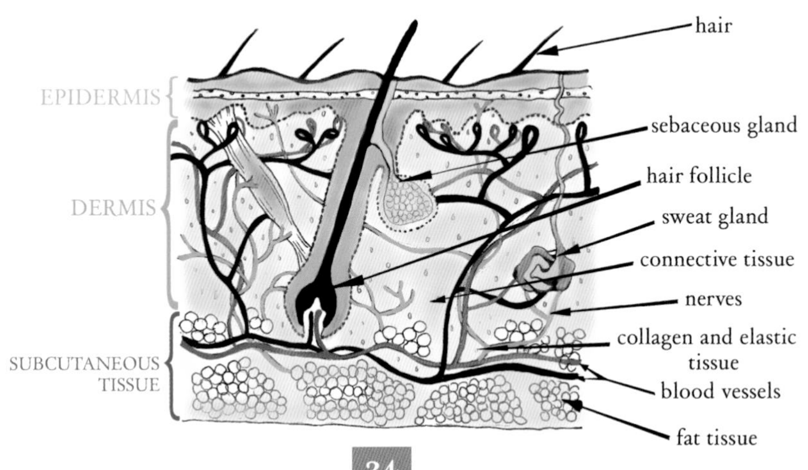

EPIDERMIS

This outer layer of skin is what you see when you look in the mirror. Its main functions are to protect the body against infections and harmful environmental factors such as the sun, to prevent too much water from seeping through your skin, and—the most obvious—to act as the glue that holds your body together. It's made up of five layers:

Stratum Corneum

This is the outermost layer of skin and is found all over the body. It's the layer to which we apply lotions and creams. The cells here are constantly being shed and are washed away for good when you exfoliate.

Stratum Lucidum

You'll find this layer in only the thicker parts of skin, like the kind on your feet and the palms of your hands; it provides extra protection to the body.

Stratum Granulosum

This thin layer of skin aids in the production of keratin, the main protein in skin.

Stratum Spinosum

Keratin production begins here.

Stratum Basale

This layer is in charge of regenerating your skin cells (so you don't shed away!). It's also where melanocytes—the cells that produce melanin (the pigment that colors your skin tone, hair color, and eye color)—are found. And it acts as the border between the epidermis and the dermis.

Shedding Pounds . . . of Skin

Next time you're complaining about your diet du jour, think of this: Humans shed about 600,000 particles of skin every hour—about 1.5 pounds a year. By 70 years old, an average person will have lost 105 pounds of skin. No calorie counting necessary!

DERMIS

Beneath the epidermis lies the dermis, where you have all your receptors for senses of touch and heat. Its thickness can exceed 3 millimeters in certain areas, such as on your back. In the dermis you'll find elements that are common to the epidermis layer, like nerves and blood vessels, but the dermis also has hair follicles and sweat glands, which are not found in any other layer of the skin. The dermis contains different types of fibers that give it a layered structure:

Collagen

This is a fibrous protein that supports other tissues in the body, making them firm and strong.

Connective Tissue

This connective fiber is what gives skin its strength and stretchiness.

QUESTIONS and Answers

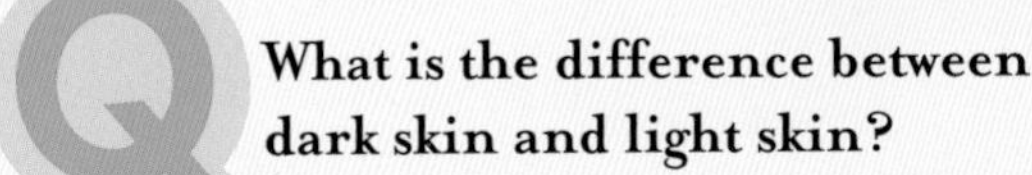

Q: What is the difference between dark skin and light skin?

A: Your skin contains something called melanin. Essentially, it's a pigment that colors your skin tone, hair color, and eye color. The more melanin you have in your skin, the darker your skin. Melanin also protects the skin against UV rays by absorbing them so the darker you are, the better your skin is protected from the sun.

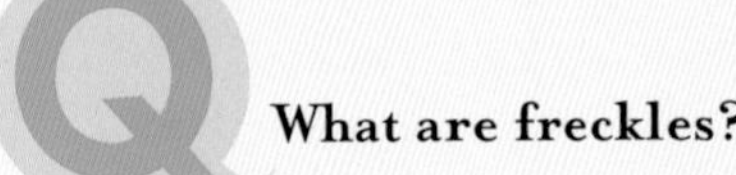

Q: What are freckles?

A: Freckles are a cluster of melanin-producing cells (melanocytes) that stick together and form those uniquely you little spots. Freckles, unlike moles, only show up after the skin has been exposed to the sun. Moles, on the other hand, can show up right after birth. Freckles usually appear on skin in two ways. For some people, their freckles get darker with sun exposure and tend to fade in the winter when not regularly exposed to sun. For others, their freckles stay the same color, can be seen all the time, and don't fade regardless of sun exposure.

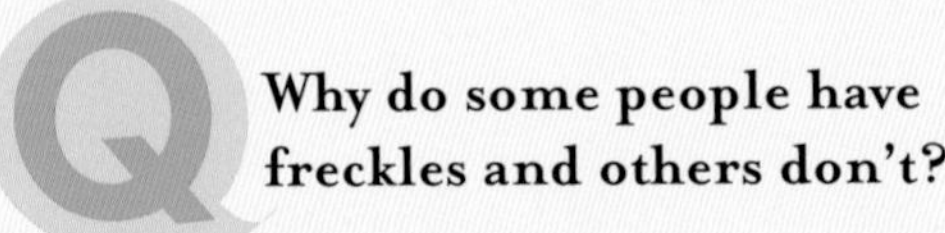

Q: Why do some people have freckles and others don't?

A: Genetics. The more people in your family with freckles, the likelier you are to have them.

Reticular Fibers

These fibers create a mesh-like netting for support and elasticity.

SUBCUTANEOUS TISSUE

This last layer of the skin is basically made up of connective tissue and fat, and contains larger nerves and blood vessels. It helps regulate your body temperature.

> **real-life elastic man**
>
> Garry Turner of Caistor, Lincolnshire, England, holds the record for the stretchiest skin, according to the Guinness World Records. He can stretch the skin on his stomach up to 6.25 inches!

What causes goose bumps?

A: Everyone has what are called arrector pili muscles. These muscles are attached to your hair follicles, which project out of your skin at an angle. When these muscles contract—because you've been scared by something or are suddenly cold—the follicles respond by literally standing up at an angle that's perpendicular to your skin.

We call them goose bumps because when a goose's feathers get plucked, they have a similar reaction that results in funny bumps.

I have little bumps that look kind of like chicken skin all over my arms. They are not goose bumps because they are there all the time and are not triggered by being cold. What are they? And should I be worried?

A: You may have something called keratosis pilaris (or KP). It's super common and affects 50 percent to 80 percent of adolescents worldwide. As with most things, there is a spectrum of severity. You can have a very mild case (which looks like goose bumps that don't go away), or a more severe case (which looks like solid, rashlike bumps). It's basically just the buildup of keratin (a protein found in your skin, nails, and hair) that gets all clogged up in your hair follicles. One way to smooth the bumps is to use a moisturizer that has glycolic or lactic acid in it. If that still doesn't work, you might want to pay a visit to your dermatologist or other skin care expert.

CHAPTER 3

The Dreaded "A"

Got acne? You're not alone. All of us at some point will wake up, look in the mirror, and find a bright red dot that decided to pop up in the middle of the night. Some people will wake up and see 20 of them. Some people will be put through the acne wringer in their early teens; others will think they've been spared, only to be hit in their adult years. It's not fun, that's for sure, but in a lot of ways it's a rite of passage.

Acne is not limited to your face, either. You can also get it on your neck, chest, back, and shoulders. (Fun!) And while teenagers definitely get hit the hardest, adults can still get it all the way into their forties—and sometimes beyond.

THE INS AND OUTS OF ZITS

Acne is like the world's worst house guest that you simply can't get to leave. And while you probably know firsthand what it is, understanding how it works is the key to diminishing its unwanted visits to your face.

Contrary to what some think, acne is (thankfully) not contagious nor is it caused by lazy personal hygiene. While there are many factors that can exacerbate acne (like stress, pollution, and hormones) one element plays a big role: a bacteria known as *Propionibacterium acnes*—or, in layman's terms, *P. acnes*.

P. Acnes

This little bacteria resides inside everyone's skin (even in those enviable people who seem to have perfect skin). It lives in an air-free environment at the bottom of your pores, and it produces enzymes that eat your skin's excess oil, which helps to balance out your skin. But when there is too much oil, the bacteria overeats, and it grows out of control. The result: a pimple.

birth control pill for zit control?

In some cases, the birth control pill is prescribed for acne. It can help because it keeps your hormones more balanced, and excessive hormonal activity is one of the greatest contributors to breakouts—especially around the time of your period.

So, is this a good option for you? It depends. Each individual reacts differently. Some people complain about weight gain, moodiness, and exhaustion, while others rave about their clear skin and crampless, more regular periods. Do a little research yourself and have a heart-to-heart with your doctor to find out if you should try it.

And remember: If you are using the birth control pill for acne, that doesn't mean you should automatically consider using it for actual *birth control*. If you are thinking about doing that, talk to your doctor first because it's not necessarily the best option: It's not 100 percent effective, and it will *not* protect you against sexually transmitted diseases.

What to Call It

Want a name for that special breed of pimple that likes to claim your face as its own? Here's a breakdown of what different zits are called.

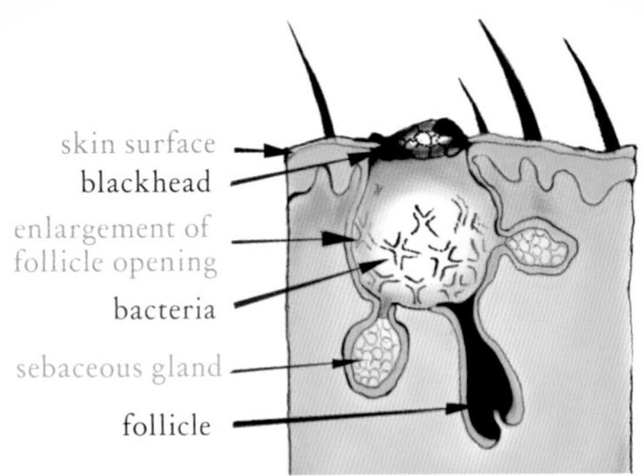

Blackhead: A non-inflamed skin pore filled with a black-colored plug at the surface. The plug is a mixture of oil and dead skin cells, and if you squeeze a blackhead, you'll notice that this mixture becomes white or yellowish when exposed to air. A blackhead is also known as an open comedone.

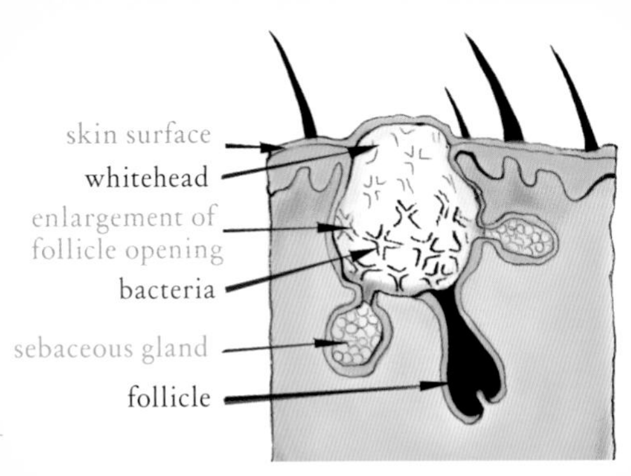

Whitehead: A small, non-inflamed skin pore filled with skin debris, bacteria, and oil. It has a little white head (as per its name) and is also known as a closed comedone.

Cyst: An inflamed and pus-filled bump that can sometimes be painful. Once one develops, it can be a recurrent problem and is normally a marker for severe acne. A cyst typically requires effective and timely treatment.

Pustule: This is what people usually refer to as a zit or a pimple. It occurs when a small collection of skin cells and oil clogs a pore. Then bacteria and inflammatory cells mobilize behind the clog and lead to a formation of pus. The pore then gets inflamed as white blood cells make their way into the follicle in order to fight bacteria. A pustule is usually kind of big and puffy.

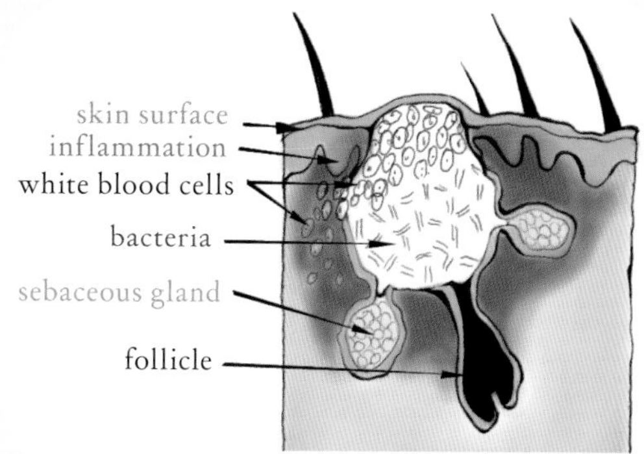

Milia: Sometimes misdiagnosed as a rash or pimples, milia are teeny, tiny white bumps. They form when dead skin cells get stuck in small pockets on the skin. You can distinguish them from whiteheads because they don't have poppable heads that are begging to be squeezed.

AT THE DOC

So you've got a bumpy mole that looks weird or an acne cyst that just won't go away. It's probably time for a doctor's visit. Normally, going to the doctor is a groan-inducing experience and conjures up images of scary needles and cold tools just jonesing to poke and prod you. But going to the dermatologist isn't, and shouldn't be, scary. Here's what to do for a first-time visit:

1. Make an appointment and go with a parent (especially if you're under 18). Prepare to answer a lot of questions like, "Why are you here?" "What are your skin concerns?" "What is your current skin care routine?" "Would you rather use topical medication or oral medication, like pills?"

2. Have an opinion on what you are willing to do (say, cleanse, exfoliate, and moisturize) and what you're not willing to do (perhaps nightly at-home masks and daily pills).

   Remember that you'll also have time after the appointment to research the various treatment options you were offered.

3. If you have an immediate problem that needs to be taken care of (infectious rash, painful cyst, severe acne), be prepared for the dermatologist to send you for some blood tests, do some extraction (zit-popping) work, or give you an injection of something like cortisone, to make a cyst diminish.

4. Talk to the dermatologist so that you two can establish a regimen that will both fit your lifestyle and yield complexion-improving results.

THE ACNE REPORT CARD

Acne is a clever beast. It can be a sly, silent intruder that attacks when you least expect it, or it can be a legion of loud soldiers who declare battle using little red bumps as ammunition. Because acne is such a chameleon, you're going to have an incredibly difficult time formulating one, guaranteed defense strategy. But one way to tackle it is to know what you're dealing with. Dermatologists use classifications of acne that are divided into four grades. See where you fit in.

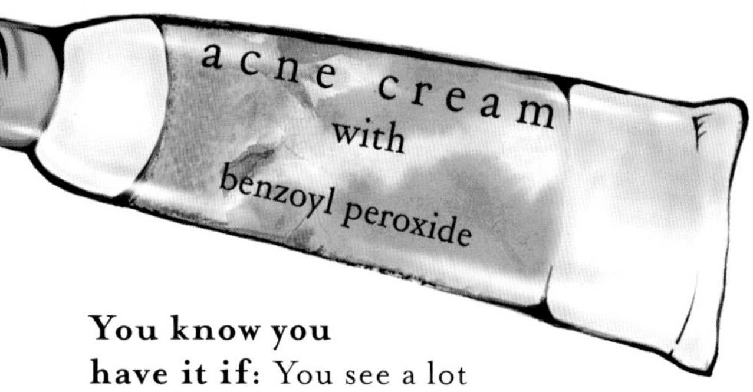

Grade 1

What it is: The mildest form of active acne commonly seen in preteens and teens, Grade 1 acne is mostly found on the nose and/or forehead. Because there is little-to-no inflammation or pain, dermatologists refer to this kind as comedonal (as opposed to inflammatory) acne.

You know you have it if: You get minor pimples that pop up every once in a while, or high concentrations of blackheads in a particular cluster.

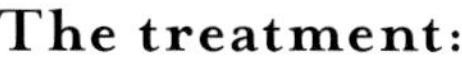

The treatment: Over-the-counter products that contain salicylic acid are a popular solution. A professional peel with glycolic or salicylic acid can also be helpful. Other skin care experts recommend tea tree oil for a natural alternative.

Grade 2

What it is: This is a slightly more intense form of acne that includes an aspect of inflammation and spreads beyond the nose and forehead.

You know you have it if: You see a lot of blackheads and whiteheads as well as a smattering of red bumps.

The treatment: Products that contain salicylic acid or benzoyl peroxide are an option and, if chosen, should be used on a daily basis to treat the affected areas. Ideally, you should use both to reap the benefits of each item. If you've tried that and feel you need something stronger, you could see a dermatologist, who may give you a prescription for a retinoid medication (like Retin-A). Retinoids are medications derived from vitamin A, and they can work wonders on the skin.

everyone's got it

Acne is the most common skin disease treated by physicians and is said to affect more than 85 percent of young adults.

know your meds

No matter which method of medication you opt for—and even if it's prescribed by a doc—you should be aware of what you're taking. This means asking questions, doing your own research, and exploring other options. Cortisone, for example, can be a very helpful medication to assist in dealing with everything from cystic acne to dermatitis. But, in rare cases, people are allergic to it; others find that if they use it too much, their skin gets used to it and the medication loses its effect. Antibiotics taken over long periods of time can also be harmful to some people, causing intestinal problems or yeast infections. And when using certain medications, like Retin-A, you need to be extra careful about sun exposure.

Be sure to talk to your doctor or pharmacist about possible side effects, so if you see something weird pop up, you will know to discontinue the meds. Also, know the exact dosage and times you're supposed to take your medicine—they won't do their job if you just take them randomly.

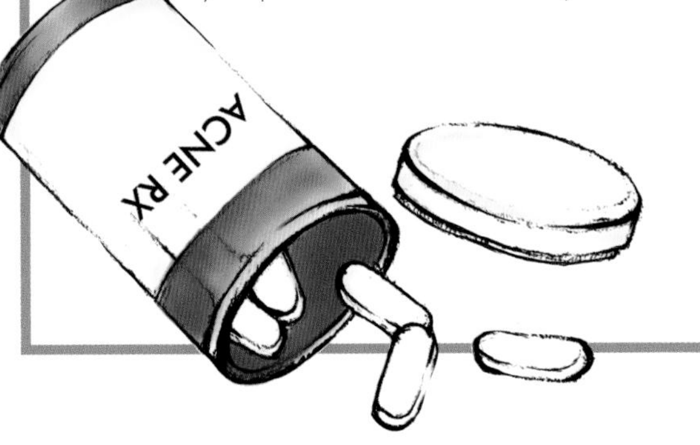

Grade 3

What it is: Moderate inflammatory acne that is irritated and may contain a lot of pus.

You know you have it if: You have several red and irritated pimples (the kind that you want to pop, even though you know you shouldn't!), in addition to the smatterings of blackheads and whiteheads you get with grades 1 and 2. You may also start to notice or feel some cystic acne forming.

The treatment: This form of acne is usually treated by a dermatologist and involves a one-two punch of various topical treatments—both over-the-counter and prescription—and occasionally an oral medication.

Grade 4

What it is: The most severe form of acne, this is called cystic acne and has a high incidence of scarring.

You know you have it if: You get harsh breakouts that include everything in the first three grades, as well as major inflammation, redness, and painful subsurface cysts.

The treatment: A visit to the dermatologist is probably your safest bet. Because this acne is so unpredictable, the only thing that seems to help is a combo of topical prescription creams like a retinoid coupled with oral antibiotics and—in severe cases—Accutane, an oral medication that is categorized as an isotretinoin. Like Retin-A, Accutane is also a vitamin A derivative, but it's way stronger.

PREVENTION IS KEY

Products with benzoyl peroxide or salicylic acid are great for treating acne, but they can also be used preventatively. Because acne naturally waxes and wanes, you'll have some days where your pimples seem to retreat and others where zits seem to be in full throttle. Use that in-between time effectively by keeping up with at-home cleansers and moisturizers that have these ingredients. Give your new routine about two months before you decide to love it or leave it.

back acne

As if getting it on your face isn't bad enough, but then you also have to get it on your back? Back acne, aka bacne, is also caused by *P. acnes*. It is typically aggravated by large amounts of sweat and oil that sit on the back for long periods of time without being cleansed, and it can be made worse by the friction between your clothing and skin, especially if you wear athletic gear or carry a heavy backpack on your shoulders.

In order to prevent those bumps from popping up, make sure you thoroughly wash your back after you've shampooed and conditioned your hair (sometimes it's your emollient conditioner that stuffs up your pores and leaves them oilier than normal). Also, if you get a sudden outbreak of back acne, you might want to do some investigating in the laundry room to see if someone's been using new fabric softeners and detergents, which could be the culprits. If you already have back acne, the best treatment is the same as the treatment for face acne: a cleanser or lotion that contains glycolic acid or salicylic acid. In the shower, you can use a long scrubbing sponge to reach your back; out of the shower, most treatments come in spray form in order to provide an easy application.

PICK, PICK, PICK

If you think channeling your inner dermatologist is a good idea and often go to town on your zits, you may want to reconsider. Picking at pimples can not only irritate your current blemishes, but also incite new blemish movement beneath the surface, not to mention potentially infecting your your face with new bacteria from your fingers. On top of that, you may be left with a scar.

That said, no matter how much self-control you have, it's inevitable that at some point you're going to be plagued by a zit that you just can't help but get your hands on. So, if you must, here's how to plot out the pimple pop.

1. **Examine it:** It should be more white than red and filled with an ooze-ready white juice. If it doesn't have a black or white head ready to be extracted, hands off. The quickest way to get rid of those is a cortisone shot at the dermatologist. If that's not an option for you, use a spot treatment and be patient. Very patient.

2. **Prepare it:** If you are ready to get poppin', cut your fingernails and wash your hands thoroughly. Soak the problem spot with a warm cloth.

3. **Pop it:** Place your fingers—not your nails!—on each side of the blemish and give it one (and only one) gentle push. If you poke and poke (and poke) at it, you'll create a major traffic jam of bacteria and cells underneath the surface, which will cause a more massive blemish in the long run. You're also looking at a longer recovery and potential scarring. After one failed attempt, step away from the zit. Wait until it stops throbbing (usually about 20 minutes), then soak it with a clean, warm washcloth for a few minutes and try again. If you're *still* unsuccessful, you're probably better off leaving it alone for the night.

   If you do have success, you'll see some white-yellow fluid emerge. A small amount of blood is also to be expected.

4. **Treat it:** After you've drained your pimple sufficiently, dab it dry and apply an acne spot treatment like benzoyl peroxide.

QUESTIONS and Answers

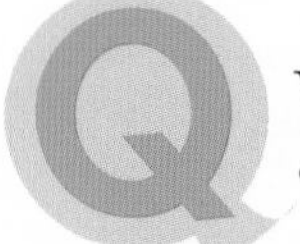

Will sunning help get rid of acne?

A: UV rays can help temporarily clear up some cases of acne. But the flip side is that too much sun increases your cancer risk, speeds up the creation of wrinkles, and alters the texture of your skin. The bottom line: Don't rely on dangerous UV rays to get rid of acne. There are lots of other treatments that have less harmful long-term effects.

Is acne caused by dirt?

A: No, it's caused by the *P. acnes* bacteria, as stated on page 31. Dirt is not one of the culprits. However, failure to wash your face properly doesn't help your case, as you're introducing external bacteria to your skin, which, when combined with *P. acnes*, can potentially spark a flare-up.

Can you get zits from eating pizza or chocolate?

A: The controversy over diet and acne rages on. Some studies say there is little or no link between the two, and others say that there is. However, the bottom line is that anyone can have a skin reaction to any food. So if you notice yourself breaking out every time you eat chocolate (or ice cream or pizza), then common sense says you should probably eat less of, or totally avoid, that food.

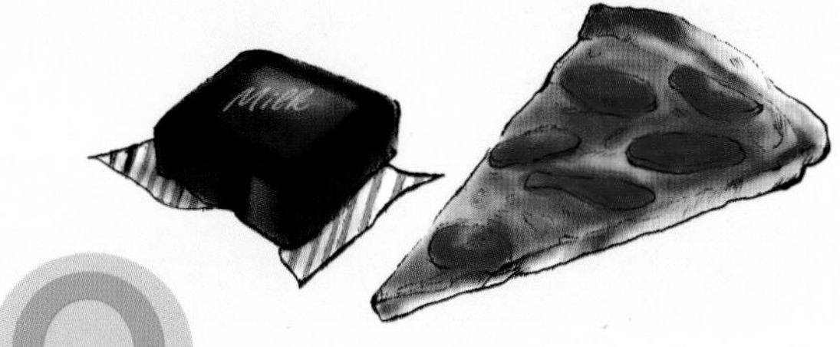

Is acne genetic?

A: Yes, the predisposition to getting acne does run in families. But if you know that you're susceptible, you can get a jump on the situation by visiting the dermatologist when you see the first signs of blemishes.

CHAPTER 4

Red Patches, Itchy Spots, and Other fun

Because the skin is such a major and complex organ, it's susceptible to all different types of ailments. So it's not uncommon to have a weird skin issue pop up. Maybe you have, at one point or another, broken out in hives after eating a strawberry, found little red dots on your arms on a hot day, or brushed flakes off your sweater while out on a date. That's all skin-related. The good news is all of this stuff is treatable. Of course, you don't want to be your own doctor and do all of your own diagnosing (as tempting as that may be), but it's good to understand the messes your skin can get itself into. Here's a quick lowdown.

CONTACT DERMATITIS (The Sudden Skin Freak-Out)

Dermatitis is a broad term that essentially just describes an inflammation of the skin. Contact dermatitis usually refers to the reaction that can occur if your skin comes into contact with something new, such as your new bubble bath.

Cause: Irritants or allergy-producing substances like detergent, metals, perfume, rubber, a weed, or even poison ivy can bring about contact dermatitis.

Treatment: First, you need to identify the cause and then stop coming into contact with it. You can use an over-the-counter hydrocortisone cream to quiet the rash, or see your doctor for something stronger if the breakout doesn't clear up. An acupuncturist or homeopath may also be able to help, if you prefer a more natural approach.

Who has it? According to the American Academy of Allergy, Asthma, and Immunology, contact dermatitis warranted more than 5 million US doctor's office visits in 2007.

DANDRUFF (The Science of Flakes)

Everyone knows about dandruff, that not-so-glamorous scalp condition that causes tiny flakes of skin to fall from your head, eliminating your ability to wear dark clothing unless you want to look like you were just out in the snow. It's easy to know if you have dandruff—it shows up in the shedding of white flakes and an itchy, irritated scalp.

Cause: Many things can create dry skin: not shampooing enough, sensitivity to hair care products, or seborrheic dermatitis (a flaky condition that occurs on especially oily parts of the body). But the most common cause of dandruff is a yeastlike fungus called malassezia furfur that feasts on your scalp. This fungus can camp out on plenty of healthy scalps, but if it grows too big, it triggers the creation of new cells on your scalp that grow too quickly, forcing the old cells to die and flake off. As they're jumping ship from your scalp, they get lumped in with sebum (oil) from your hair, which makes them snowball into white crumblike pieces. This fungus can pop up on dry scalps, as well as oily scalps, and things like a poor diet (that includes too many sugary carbs) and stress can aggravate the yeast.

Treatment: Start by simplifying your hair care routine by using fewer and gentler products. You can also try using a deep conditioner to see if dry skin is the culprit. If none of this works, try a medicated shampoo (see page 44 for different options), which may help if malassezia furfur is in fact causing your dandruff. Finally, you may want to limit your intake of sugar—bread, alcohol, and sweets—because these foods are thought by some to create a playground for yeast. Instead, reach for foods like soybeans, bananas, avocados, nuts, and dark leafy greens, which are high in the skin-healthy vitamin B.

Who has it? Though it's tough to estimate (not everyone goes to the doctor or shouts it from the rooftops if they're afflicted), some studies project that 40 percent of people have dandruff.

which shampoo is for you?

One of the most common types of dandruff is the kind caused by the yeastlike fungus malassezia furfur. When a fungus is afoot, an effective way of tackling it is with a medicated shampoo. Here's a cheat sheet of what's out there.

IF YOU HAVE:
mild itching and flaking

TRY: Shampoos with zinc pyrithione, an antibacterial superhero ingredient that can help kill the fungus.

IF YOU HAVE:
lots of flaking

TRY: Tar-based shampoos, which can delay the process of cell reproduction (i.e., flaking).

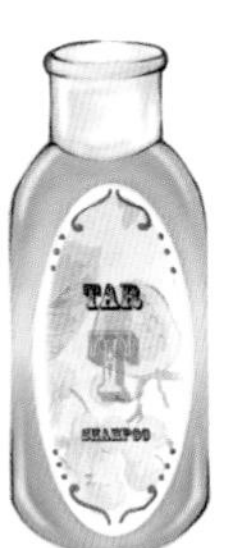

IF YOU HAVE:
mild flaking and oily hair

TRY: Shampoos with salicylic acid. Yep, the same miracle ingredient that helps fight acne can help beat dandruff too. Essentially, it exfoliates the scales that form on your scalp, which are made up of extra skin cells and clumped-together oil. Once those extra scales have been eliminated, the dandruff will subside.

IF YOU HAVE:
severe dandruff and non-color-treated hair

TRY: Selenium sulfide shampoos. Said to be a major soldier against malassezia furfur, these shampoos can decrease the yeast. Just be careful if you have highlighted hair—this ingredient can sometimes damage the color.

IF YOU HAVE:
severe dandruff and nothing else has worked

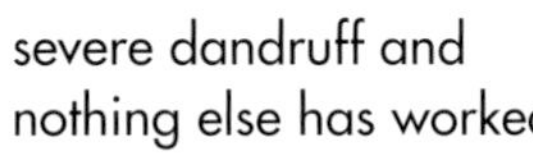

TRY: Shampoos with ketoconazole. This ingredient is a powerful antifungal agent that's available over the counter and by prescription.

IF YOU HAVE:
any of the above, but want to try something natural

TRY: A shampoo with tea tree oil. Tea tree oil is a natural antifungal that's derived from a plant native to Australia. In addition to fighting fungus, it also clears sebaceous glands that are clogged up with bacteria, leading some experts to suggest that it could be a viable acne treatment as well.

THE HIVES
(Itch, Itch, Scratch)

Hives, or as they're known under their more science-y name, urticaria, are itchy pink swellings that occur on the skin and last less than 24 hours. In some cases, you might get these kind of swellings repeatedly over days, weeks, or even months. Hives are typically not a big deal and will usually clear up within six weeks or so. If your hives hang on longer, that might mean they are from a fungal or viral infection, or from an unknown allergy or even stress.

Cause: Docs won't always know exactly why you got them, but hives, which typically come on pretty quickly, can usually be traced back to something you just came in contact with—a type of food, pollen, insect bite, a drug or chemical, animal dander, or even a piece of clothing. Luckily, the allergic reaction can be easily dealt with once the allergy is detected. Other times, the cause for urticaria remains unknown; in those cases, it often goes away eventually and no one ever knows what caused it.

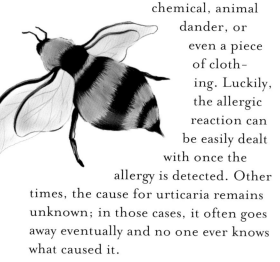

Experts have drawn up a list of the foods that most commonly cause a hive reaction: shellfish, chocolate, nuts, tomatoes, eggs, berries, and milk. If you get hives, investigate if it might be one of these. While most hives are just uncomfortable or annoying, there are times when there's cause for concern. If you experience even *one* of the below symptoms, call the doctor!

- swollen tongue
- facial swelling (particularly around the cheek area)
- swelling of your throat that makes breathing difficult, otherwise known as anaphylaxis
- dizziness
- asthmatic wheezing

Treatment: Generally speaking, you can take care of a minor hive outbreak by avoiding whatever you think might have caused the hives. Been hanging around the neighbor's new pet kitty? Tried shellfish for the first time? Think about what you may have exposed yourself to—particularly anything new or different—that could have triggered the hives and avoid it altogether to see if they go away.

In the short-term, an over-the-counter antihistamine can calm hives. Hydrocortisone is also a good go-to; but use caution and read the instructions with an eagle-eye, as it should only be used for short spurts of time.

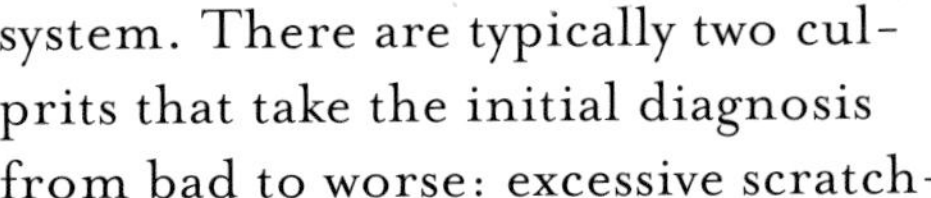

Who has it?
According to the American Academy of Dermatology, an estimated 10 percent to 20 percent of Americans will experience at least one case of hives in their lifetime.

ECZEMA (The Moody Skin Disease)

Eczema has many forms, but its most common form is also known as atopic dermatitis, and it is essentially a very fickle, very moody rash that seems to appear for no reason, tethered to no real trigger. It has also been called the "itch that rashes" since it often starts with just an itch and the rash appears later.

Cause: Though the cause of this disorder is unknown, docs think it may have something to do with having a combination of dry, sensitive skin and an imbalance in the immune system. There are typically two culprits that take the initial diagnosis from bad to worse: excessive scratching and stress. Either can lead to red, swollen cracking clusters of skin that then form a fluidlike crusting on top of the affected area.

Treatment: One thing you can do to treat eczema is to moisturize with creams (not lotions—they won't hydrate as intensively) that are fragrance free and contain ceramides, which will help repair the skin barrier. The FDA has also approved moisturizers that contain colloidal oatmeal as an agent to soothe irritation.

If that doesn't work, a doc might prescribe a topical cortisone cream, or an antihistamine as a last resort. Acupuncture and Chinese herbs have also been shown in some studies to help certain types of eczema; it could be a good option if nothing else is working, or if you'd rather not take medications.

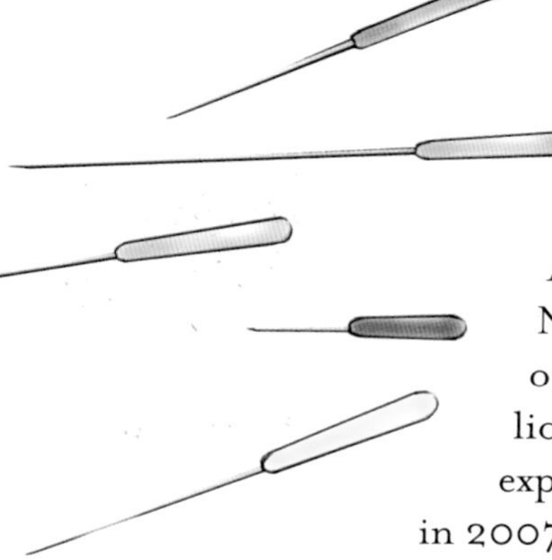

Who has it? According to the National Institutes of Health, 15 million Americans experienced eczema in 2007.

HEAT RASH (Not So Hot!)

It's a hot day and you are all set to wear that bikini—except that you can already feel the little red dots all over your arms, back, and chest. You have heat rash. Also known as prickly heat or miliaria, heat rash appears in red clusters of rashlike pimples when your skin is overheating.

Cause: It usually happens in hot, overly humid surroundings when your body begins to sweat excessively. The sweat glands become blocked under something (like tight-fitting clothes); it's that trapped perspiration that results in teeny bumps on your skin. If and when those bumps pop, you might feel a tingling burn, or a heat that feels prickly, as suggested in the name.

Treatment: When you see heat rash appear, apply a cold compress to the area. Normally this common skin condition will go away on its own, with a little help from some temperature regulation. Also, some experts recommend taking a bath and then using an unscented talcum powder or baking soda to help absorb the extra moisture. If the rash still feels hot to the touch, pick up some calamine lotion for a cooling effect.

Who has it? There haven't been lots of studies that have documented cases, but, suffice it to say, it is very common.

PSORIASIS [SORE-EYE-AH-SIS] (Too Many Skin Cells)

Psoriasis is a skin condition that relates to accelerated skin cell turnover. It means your epidermal cells turn over every few days as opposed to once a month, so the skin is like an overactive factory, churning out too many new cells before the body can get rid of the old ones. The result: a collision that looks like scaly skin, and red lesions covered with a silvery, white crust. Lovely, right?

reflexology to combat skin issues?

Reflexology is the act of applying pressure to certain parts of the hands and feet to treat pain or illness elsewhere in the body. There have been limited studies about reflexology's effectiveness, but some believe that it can help treat skin issues. How? Reflexologists believe that skin issues arise when the body cannot get rid of toxins through internal organs (because they aren't functioning properly) and instead tries to get rid of them via the skin (leading to things like eczema). Reflexology is said to put the internal organs back to work by affecting their pressure sensors; in return, the toxins get flushed out the right way—and skin conditions are said to clear up.

Cause: Psoriasis is believed to occur because of a genetic malfunction in the immune system, though environmental factors may also contribute. Flare-ups are unpredictable, yet many teens and twentysomethings believe their breakout occurred after a bout of strep throat or a different infection of some sort, like an ear ache or bronchitis.

Treatment: Docs will prescribe topical steroid treatments in combination with creams that contain salicylic acid and coal tar to slow down the skin's excessive production. For more severe cases, light therapy or a series of prescription pills or injections are used. People looking for a more natural approach can try over-the-counter herbal remedies, or those prescribed by a naturopath or Chinese medicine doctor.

Who has it? According to the National Institutes of Health, as many as 7.5 million Americans have psoriasis, and 75 percent of all cases develop before the patient is 40.

ROSACEA (ROH-ZAY-SHA) (The Red Monster)

If you're finding that your face gets red easily and often (and not from crushing over that new guy in school), and if you notice something that looks like a little colony of pimples popping up on your nose, cheeks, chin, and forehead, you may have what's called rosacea. It can be uncomfortable and make your skin feel like it's experiencing a stinging sensation, and it can make your eyes feel itchy and dry.

Cause: Rosacea happens when the blood vessels in the face widen more than usual. The surplus of blood near the skin's surface causes that blushed appearance. Things like alcohol, spicy foods, and stress can trigger an outbreak.

Studies have also found that it is genetic. In other words, if Grandma has red, splotchy patches on her skin—particularly after just one glass of wine—there's a good chance you might have it, too. According to the National Rosacea Society, approximately 40 percent of rosacea patients could name a relative who had similar symptoms.

Treatment: If you are diagnosed with rosacea, docs will tell you to try to avoid any triggers. They may also prescribe an antibiotic prescription cream or pills (to calm the inflammation) or a powerful vitamin A derivative cream (like Retin-A).

Who has it? In 2008, it was estimated that at least 13 million cases were diagnosed, but docs believe this number to be even higher based on the frequency with which this condition goes undetected or misdiagnosed. Rosacea is most commonly found in patients between the ages of 25 and 70 and is much more common in those with milky-white skin. While the statistics show that women are more likely to get rosacea, the more severe cases are diagnosed in guys.

famous face

Although it may seem like most celebs were born with perfect skin (or at least have it thanks to the art of airbrushing), there are a few stars on red alert with this skin affliction. Comedienne and sometimes TV hostess Rosie O'Donnell has spoken often about her battle with rosacea. And for another piece of proof that the occasional outbreak can't hold you back: the 42nd president of the United States of America, William Jefferson Clinton, has it.

QUESTIONS and Answers

I have a gross cold sore and it hurts. How do I get rid of it and prevent it from coming back?

A: The first time a cold sore rears its ugly head, it can last for up to two or three weeks. Bummer. Bigger bummer? It tends to come back. These recurring cold sores, which are viral infections also known as HSV (herpes simplex virus), disappear within three to seven days. To avoid or limit future breakouts, keep your lip tissue as healthy as possible. Limit triggers like sun exposure, dry lips, and stress—and use plenty of lip balm with sunscreen in it.

When you do get a cold sore, you can try an ointment with an analgesic, also known as a painkiller, to help relieve pain and aid with soreness. If your outbreaks are really bad, try a prescription medication (Acyclovir, Valtrex, or Famvir) to speed up the healing process—and sometimes even eliminate outbreaks (though the virus stays in your blood). You should also be forewarned: Herpes spreads easily through close physical contact. If you have cold sores on your mouth, you can spread them to others (or catch them from others) through kissing and oral sex; if you have herpes on your genitals, you can also spread or catch them through oral sex and intercourse. The virus can also spread when you don't have symptoms, but you can limit the chances of contagion by not engaging in any close physical contact when you or your honey has an outbreak.

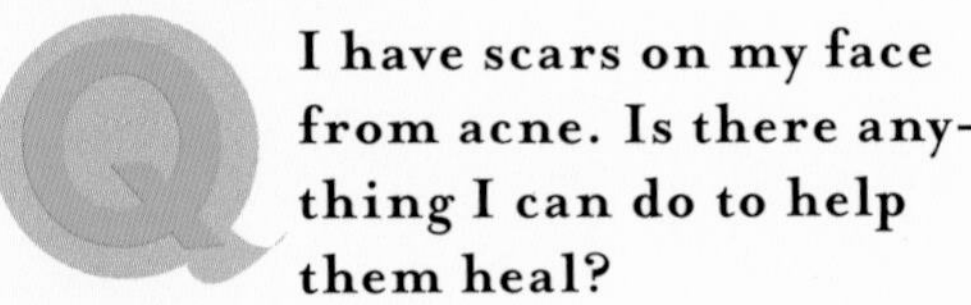

I have scars on my face from acne. Is there anything I can do to help them heal?

A: First off, it's good to know the difference between a red mark and a scar. Technically a scar is a permanent mark caused by some damage to the skin. It can appear as an indentation or as a raised bump on the skin's surface. It's an actual alteration of the skin's structure. A red mark is simply that, a discoloration that appears when the skin is healing.

A good way to tell the difference is to feel—not just look—at the spot in question. If it's just a red mark—lucky you!—that will go away over time. And, in the meantime, you can dab on a cream that contains onion bulb extract, also known as allium cepa, which has been shown to help lighten up the red.

For actual scars, some studies show that laser or light therapies administered at the dermatologist's office can make a significant improvement on marked-up skin; other health professionals advise the use of vitamin E. Talk to your skin care professional to see what he or she thinks is best for your type of scar. Also, check out page 90 in Chapter Eight for advice on how to best cover up scars.

alternative solutions

Visiting a physician is still how most people in the US address health problems, but lots of people are now also trying other skin care experts like naturopaths, acupuncturists, facialists, or homeopaths—and getting good results. And many people find that a combination of approaches works best. Do a little research, ask a lot of questions, and see what works for you. Like mostly everything else in your life, skin care is not a one-size-fits-all endeavor.

CHAPTER 5

Tweeze It, Wax It, Shave It

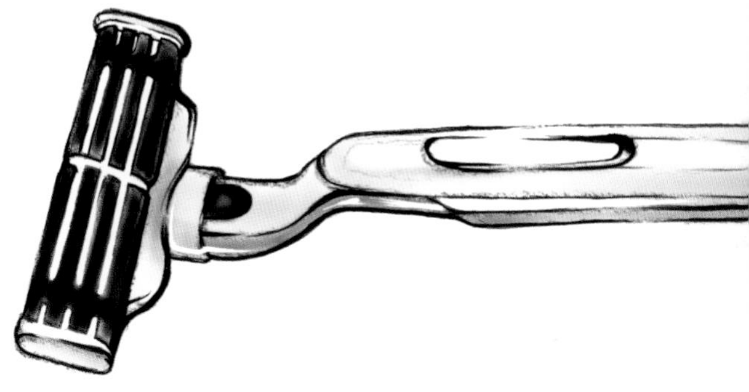

Having hair in places you'd rather not is a fact of life for most people. Why can't it just grow where it's supposed to? And for those who decide to remove it, your options—razors, lasers, hot wax, secret chemical formulas, tiny plierlike tools—are most definitely sci-fi worthy. Depending on your skin type, budget, and threshold for pain, some courses of action work better than others. Here's a list (in A-Z order) of the most common hair removal practices. See which methods might be best for you.

DEPILATORY

What it is:

A cream or gel chemical formula containing one of two key ingredients: calcium thioglycolate or sodium thioglycolate. You lather it on and leave it for about five minutes (or as otherwise directed on the box), depending on the product. The chemicals dissolve the hair protein, and the hair withers up and is easily wiped off.

Use it on:

Legs, underarms, bikini, and face. (If you use it on your face, get a product that is meant for the gentle skin there and be sure to try a patch test first to make sure.)

Who it works best for:

Depilatories are best for people who want to take small to larger-sized patches of hair off at the surface level without using a razor. If, however, your hair is thick and grows back rapidly, this might not be your best option. It's messy and time-consuming, and putting chemicals on your body two or three times a week—especially over a large section of your body—just isn't ideal.

Ouch factor:

Low. The smell, on the other hand, can be intense. While every product is different and the technologies have improved, there's still a bit of a stink—especially if you're using the product while all cooped up in your bathroom.

How it treats your skin:

Do a patch test before you use it to test your skin's tolerance. Most products come with their own post-treatment lotion to leave skin smooth. If yours doesn't, try something simple, like an aloe vera lotion, that doesn't contain a heavy fragrance. If you develop a burn or rash, stop using it.

ELECTROLYSIS

What it is:

Electrical stimulation in which a needle is inserted into each follicle and the hair gets zapped. As the follicle is damaged, so is the possibility for regrowth. Though it can take several appointments with a trained professional (it can take several zaps to damage the follicle and there are lots of follicles), the procedure is safe and can result in permanent hair removal.

Use it on:

Though you can use it anywhere, it is a *slooooow* process, so it's most effective on small areas like facial hair. It could take years to do it on a leg.

Who it works best for:

Any skin type of any color is eligible for this method.

Ouch aspect:

Needles and electricity (even in a safe, small dose) do not make for a spalike experience, but you'll live through it.

How it treats your skin:

You may experience some pain, redness, or discomfort, but that should subside within 24 hours. If it persists beyond that, you should see a doctor.

LASER HAIR REMOVAL

What it is:

Laser hair removal (also referred to as laser hair reduction, because it really lessens the amount of hair you have but does not permanently remove it all) works by sending laser beams into your hair follicle, producing heat in the follicle, which then burns hair at the root. That in turn, inhibits regrowth.

ingrown hairs

Ingrown hair is hair that gets stuck beneath the skin and grows under because it can't break through. As the hair grows, the surrounding skin swells and can even get infected. To treat ingrown hairs, buff the skin in a circular motion, which may thin the skin and lift the hair out from under its lump. Or ask your aesthetician to lift them out for you at your next waxing appointment. If you have a lot of ingrown hairs, see a dermatologist, who may extract them.

Laser hair removal can be pricey, and you need a whole slew of visits, but it's a safe and effective technology, and the end result is way less hair and little to no need for shaving and waxing.

Use it on:

Legs, arms, bikini, chest, back, nipples—pretty much anywhere. You can also use it on your face, but the hair there tends to be a little thinner and lighter, and therefore doesn't work as well as areas that have darker, thicker hair.

Who it works best for:

Laser hair removal is good for those who want to remove hair from large patches of the body since the laser acts on several hairs at once. The current lasers are best for someone with dark, thick wiry hair and fair to medium skin tone, because the efficacy of the laser depends on how well it can distinguish between the skin and hair color. (The laser finds the hair, heats up its root, and subsequently burns it off. If your skin color is too close to the color of your hair, the laser may get confused and burn your skin along with the hair follicle.) New lasers have recently been developed for people with darker skin; if that's you, keep an eye out for them, as they're coming into regular use across the country.

Ouch aspect:

It feels like quick, stinging twinges of pain—like someone snapping a rubber band on your skin—over and over again along the area. It can also burn a bit, but generally the pain does not last.

How it treats your skin:

For most people, laser hair removal can actually improve skin quality. For people who have damaged skin (ingrown hairs, red blotches, or rough bumps), the laser can help smooth it out and exfoliate it.

SHAVING

What it is:

Shaving is the cheapest (short term, anyway), quickest, and easiest hair removal process. It is the removal of hair by cutting it down to the level of the skin with a razor. Much to the comfort of many a beach-bound girl, shaving can be done quickly in your shower and get you ready for that bikini, miniskirt, or running outfit in a matter of minutes. Only downside: It never ends. If you choose shaving over these other options, you're a lifer.

Use it on:

Legs, underarms, and bikini.

shaving tips

- ✔ Change blades frequently: A dull blade can lead to more nicks and cuts.
- ✔ Start at your ankles and shave upward, against the grain of the growth.
- ✔ Wet your skin preshave; it will soften the area and make maneuvering the razor easier.
- ✔ Be sure to rinse the razor head in hot water immediately after each stroke to get more mileage out of the blade.

Who it works best for:

Everyone can shave, but those with finer hair will do better as the stubble will be less aggressive. If you have über-sensitive skin, opt for a gentle shaving gel or cream.

Ouch aspect:

Shaving itself doesn't typically hurt at all, though almost everyone gets a cut from time to time.

How it treats your skin:

Some people respond great to shaving, and others get shaving rashes, irritation, and even ingrown hairs. For people with sensitive skin, shaving every day can be problematic; when the blade glides over your skin, you're not only removing hair but also exfoliating that top dead layer of skin cells, which can leave sensitive or dry skin feeling raw. Always keep skin well moisturized postshave (and don't exfoliate your legs preshave).

TWEEZING

What it is:

The removal of hair with teeny metal forceps, which draws hair out at the root.

Use it on:

Eyebrows and random hairs that pop up on your body.

Who it works best for:

Everyone.

tweezing tips

- ✔ To keep your brows even, make sure whatever you do to one, you do to the other, too.
- ✔ Pull out just one hair at a time.
- ✔ Don't moisturize right before, it can make gripping the hair difficult.

Ouch aspect:

It's a fleeting pain that goes away in only a few seconds.

How it treats your skin:

This method seems to be the least aggressive on your skin, and though some sensitive types might experience redness, that slight irritation will disappear shortly. Some people do get ingrown hairs from tweezing.

WAXING

What it is:

There are different types of wax. The most common is heated wax. It's spread out on an area of hair, left to cool for a moment, and then removed with a muslin cloth and a quick stroke, thereby ripping hair out at the follicle.

Cold wax is obviously not heated, and it works by being spread on, patted down, and ripped off as a clump. There's no heat (and subsequently less irritation), and there's also no muslin cloth. If you have sensitive skin but can tolerate wax, this is a better way to go.

Sugaring is another form of waxing. A substance that looks like caramel is applied and peeled off quickly, much like a regular wax. The difference here is that this substance is water-soluble and easier to remove. (Wax can be a little sticky and stubborn to get off your skin.) This is also good for someone who has sensitive skin.

Use it on:

Legs, arms, bikini, face, chest, back, nipples—pretty much anywhere.

Who it works best for:

Although anyone can opt for this service, those with pale hair that is fine or sparse will experience the least amount of pain and need to make less-frequent appointments.

Ouch aspect:

Well, it ain't no walk in the park, but it is bearable. And on the upside, each time you do it it gets easier.

basic or brazilian

Before you choose a bikini line option off the waxing menu, make sure you know what you're gettin'.

BASIC BIKINI: Removes hair along the sides of the bikini area and maintains the natural, triangular shape.

BRAZILIAN: A flat-out defuzz to get rid of every possible hair, everywhere. You can ask them to leave a strip in the middle or go completely bare.

How it treats your skin:

Some people respond really well to waxing and find that their hair growth even slows over time. Others get ingrown hairs. If you do experience irritation or a large amount of ingrown hairs, choose another form of hair removal. If you're going to wax in the comfort of your own bathroom, be sure to pull your skin taught, and pull the wax off parallel and low to the body.

waxing tips

- ✔ Between appointments, shaving is a big no-no. You have to wait until the hair is at least a ¼-inch long to be gripped by the wax.
- ✔ Don't wax three days before or during the first three days of your period, when your skin is at its most sensitive.
- ✔ Don't go for a wax after you've been sunburned in that area.

QUESTIONS and Answers

Q: What do I do about those stray hairs that grow out of my chin, neck, and nipples?

A: Everyone gets these hairs, so don't think you're alone. To get rid of them, pluck them with a tweezer after you shower, when hair is softer and more pluckable. If the hairs persist, look into laser removal or electrolysis, either of which is ideal for small areas like this. You can also wax these hairs, but have a professional do it a few times before you decide to take matters into your own hands.

I have hair growing out of my mole. Can I laser that off for good?

A: Moles are the trickiest problem because there's no permanent solution to getting rid of the hair that grows out of them. It's not usually recommended to laser the hair at the sight of a mole because you can get burned. Tweezing is the way to go.

CHAPTER 6

Let the Sunshine In? Maybe Not.

It's not news that the sun can be harmful to your skin. And it's more harmful today than it was even 100 years ago. That's because the ozone layer, which helps to screen out ultraviolet rays, including dangerous UVB rays, has been depleted by pollution. That means we are all more susceptible to sun damage and need to be on top of our game when it comes to sun care.

If you are alive and breathing in the 21st century you've heard the warnings. But you may not have heeded them. It can be tempting to stay out in the sun for long periods of time, especially if you don't burn easily, but you should know all the facts.

WHAT IS SKIN CANCER?

Skin cancer makes up almost half of all diagnosed cancers in the United States, making it the most common form of the potentially deadly disease. The American Cancer Society estimates that about 60,000 cases of melanoma were diagnosed in the United States during 2007.

Skin cancer is one of the few cancers that is mostly preventable—90 percent of cases can be traced back to sun damage. And check this out: Each day, more than 20 people die from skin cancer.

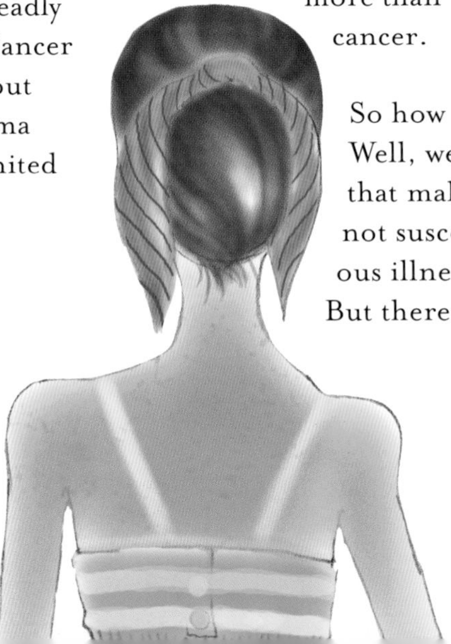

So how do you get it? Well, we all have genetic coding that makes us susceptible (or not susceptible) to getting various illnesses, like skin cancer. But there are definitely things that increase your chances of a skin cancer diagnosis. The biggest culprit is overexposure to sun rays. Research shows that even one blistering sunburn significantly increases your chances of getting skin cancer later in life. Now, that doesn't mean you should go lock yourself in a dark cave, but it does mean that you need to get sun smart, and fast.

There are two major categories of skin cancers: non-melanoma and melanoma.

NON-MELANOMA SKIN CANCER

These are much more common than melanoma, and come most often in one of these two forms: basal cell carcinoma and squamous cell carcinoma.

Basal Cell Carcinoma

This is the most common form of skin cancer (and the most common type of cancer diagnosed in America every year). It originates in the bottom layer of the epidermis.

What to look for:

- A patch of redness that suddenly appears on your skin. You're most likely to see it on your scalp, chest, arms, shoulders, or legs.
- A pink flat patch or a pink bump that often includes a scab in the center.
- An open sore that bleeds, oozes, or crusts and remains raw with no sign of healing.

what's in a mole?

Though people call all of those brownish beauty marks "moles," there are actually different kinds of moles. Typical moles are the small, brown dots or growths that can appear raised on the skin. Then there are atypical moles, also known as dysplastic nevi. These are more unusual looking and are more likely to turn cancerous.

The more moles you have, the greater your chances are of having an atypical mole, so if you get lots of them, it's good to get them checked yearly by a dermatologist. It's quick and easy, if not a little embarrassing (you have to strip down to your skivvies). But, if one of your atypical moles is detected early, it can make all the difference in preventing the development of a skin cancer.

Any of these signs could mean that you have a basal cell carcinoma, which is essentially a skin cancer that develops in the skin or in the tissue that covers organs.

Why worry? In very rare cases, this type of cancer can spread to your muscles, nerves, or bones, and will require aggressive treatment.

Who's at risk? Though basal cell carcinoma can affect anyone of any skin type, those who have fair skin and light hair are at greater risk because they are more likely to sunburn. Also at risk: Anyone who plays a sport or has a job that requires being outside for long periods; anyone who lives in a year-round sunny environment; and serious sun worshippers.

safe is the new sexy

Back in Europe and England during the Elizabethan era (1558–1603), fair-skinned ladies did not go in search of a tan. In fact, they powdered their faces alabaster white, and that porcelain complexion remained fashionable well into the Victorian era (1837–1901), when bustled-up women walked around in hats and carried parasols to avoid getting any mark of a suntan.

Somewhere along the line (modern myth cites a jet-setting Coco Chanel in the late 1920s as the start of tan-o-mania), bronze became the new look for ladies. Women were frying themselves in the sun and ultimately fake-baking in the ever-popular and wildly dangerous tanning beds. And while a tawny exterior may look de riguer, your skin—like a rebellious kid being forced to do something she doesn't want to—will retaliate and start showing signs of wrinkles or, worse yet, skin cancer.

Squamous Cell Carcinoma

This is the second most common form of skin cancer, and it affects cells that are located in the epidermis. The good news about this type of cancer is that, if detected early, treatment is hopeful. In fact, most of these cases are cured by a surgery done in a dermatologist's office.

What to look for:

- Red, scaly patches that can sometimes contain asymmetrical borders, blood, or crusting.
- An open sore that remains raw and bloody without healing.
- A raised growth that bleeds easily and appears to grow quickly.
- A wartlike growth that can bleed or form a crust.

Any of these signs could mean that you have a squamous cell carcinoma.

Why worry? If SCC isn't treated in time, there's a chance that it could spread to your lymph nodes or to other organs, which is rare but can be fatal; treatment will likely involve intense treatment such as chemotherapy and radiation.

Who's at risk? Again, people with alabaster skin and light features are most at risk, as are those who spend a lot of time in direct sunlight. For those with dark skin, these types of carcinomas can sometimes develop on burn scars.

love your lips

Lip Balm
spf 30

Lips—like the rest of your body—need sun protection. Look for ingredients in lip balms that flaunt an SPF (of 30 or higher, preferably) or a zinc oxide base. There are also sunblocks specifically made for the softer skin on your lips. Put the kibosh on petroleum jelly or any oil-based glosses, which actually attract the sun.

Melanoma Skin Cancer

Melanoma pops up far less frequently than other types of skin cancer, but it's far more lethal. It is a malignant (i.e., it's cancerous and can spread) tumor that originates in the melanocytes, the cells that produce the pigment melanin (see page 26 for more on melanin).

What to look for:
Doctors have come up with an ABCDE guide for detecting melanomas. Here's what to look for:

Asymmetry One side of your mole is different from the other.

Border Your mole has a border with uneven edges.

Color Your mole is more than one color.

Diameter Your mole is greater than 6 mm (size of a pencil eraser).

Evolving Your mole has changed in size, shape, or color.

Also: If your mole starts bleeding or oozing for no reason.

Why worry? Melanoma is a big deal, so it's imperative to catch it early. If you don't, you face the possibility of aggressive treatments and a series of surgeries to remove it from where it has spread. The treatments—like radiology and chemotherapy—can also cause a whole host of health problems. If not caught early enough, melanoma can be fatal.

Who's at risk? Those who have spent too much time baking in the sun, as well as those who started with a large number of moles, are at greatest risk. Family history also makes a big difference: One in every 10 people with melanoma had a family member who faced the same diagnosis.

say no to baking

Recent reports claim that nearly 30 million people tan indoors in the US annually and 2.3 million of them are teens. If you're thinking of becoming a regular customer at a tanning salon anytime soon, think twice about it. Excessive exposure to tanning beds before age 35 can increase your melanoma risk by a whopping 75 percent.

fake it till you make it

If a bronzed bod or lit-from-within glow is what you desire when the summer rolls around, there is a safe way to get it: self-tanning. Wondering how it works? Every self-tanner (lotion, cream, spray, towelette) contains dihydroxyacetone (DHA). DHA is a nontoxic ingredient that reacts with your skin to produce a golden brown pigment on your skin.

There are many different ways you can self-tan—at home with an over-the-counter product, at a spa where you're painted with a tanning formula, or at a booth where you're sprayed with a steady mist of the stuff.

If you are going to do it yourself, be sure to exfoliate beforehand, especially the dry areas such as your elbows and knees; this prevents the tanner from collecting on those dry areas and instead allows it to spread more evenly for a natural look. Also, you'd be wise to lounge around in dark clothes for the 24 hours after application. Many of the lotions can stain lighter duds.

And, finally, the beauty operatives are always working out the kinks and forming new technologies. If you're into self-tanning, be on the lookout for the latest and greatest in the industry.

SUN SMARTS

When out in the sun, follow these guidelines. Even when there are thick clouds or it's overcast, know that UV rays can still travel through clouds and you need protection.

- Wear a broad-spectrum sunscreen preferably SPF 30 or higher—and really lather it on. Sunscreen is an integral part of your battle against solar radiation and sun damage. In the past five years, new broad-spectrum sunscreens contain products that guard against both UVA and UVB rays. (See the Q & A section on page 69 to better understand what SPF means, and what UVA and UVB rays are.)

- Be extra careful between the hours of 10 am and 4 pm when rays are at their strongest.
- Cover up: That cute bikini you're sporting will look even cuter accessorized with a roomy caftan or fun board shorts.
- Grab those sunnies! Big Jackie O-style sunglasses with UV absorption can provide excellent protection for your sensitive eyes, not to mention fend off fine lines.

getting vitamin d

A little unprotected sun exposure—about 15 minutes a day 3 times a week—helps your body produce vitamin D, which is essential to maintaining the proper amount of calcium and phosphorous in your blood. (Some nutritionists believe that vitamin D can also lift your mood and help build stronger bones.) Just make sure you really cap it at 15 minutes; going beyond that can be harmful. Other ways to get your dose of D include eating a healthy amount of dairy products, fish, and fortified cereals, and taking a vitamin D supplement.

QUESTIONS and Answers

Q: What's the difference between UVA rays and UVB rays?

A: UVA rays are the longer UV rays that can penetrate everything from windows to light clothing. These rays are usually responsible for the aging process (wrinkling, leathering, cracking) and are less often associated with skin cancers. UVB, on the other hand, are the shorter rays that more easily cause sunburns and are most commonly associated with skin cancers.

Q: What do the SPF numbers mean, and how do I choose the right one?

A: The sun protection factor (SPF) is a number that states how long it takes for you to get a sunburn with the sunscreen on your skin, as opposed to how long it would take without the sunscreen. For example, if you are wearing SPF 30, and your skin normally gets red after 10 minutes, you can stay out in the sun 30 times 10 (or 300 minutes) before you have to reapply. This number gets compromised, however, if you go in the water or are sweating profusely. In either of those cases, you should reapply sooner.

It's important to note that the SPF measures the effect of UVB rays, but it does not measure the protection against UVA rays, so that makes this equation a little tricky. Your best bet is to use a broad-spectrum sunscreen that contains not only a UVB blocker like para-aminobenzoic acid (PABA) orbenzophenomes, but also a broad-spectrum (both UVA and UVB rays) blocker like zinc oxide, titanium dioxide, Mexoryl, or Avobenzone.

Q: What is the difference between a sunscreen with a chemical blocker and one with a physical blocker?

A: Physical blockers (like zinc oxide and titanium dioxide) reflect UV light rays; chemical blockers (like Avobenzone, oxybenzone, and Mexoryl) absorb UV light. Read the ingredients on the sunscreen bottle to find out what's inside.

Q: My moisturizer has sunscreen in it. Is that enough sun protection?

A: Yes, if your moisturizer has an SPF 30 or higher. The question, though, is whether you're applying (and reapplying) enough of it to count. To be extra safe, apply a separate sunscreen with an SPF of at least 30 under your moisturizer, especially if you're going to be outside for any length of time. Or you could just forgo the moisturizer and use the sunscreen alone—it often contains moisturizing ingredients.

Q: How often do I need to apply sunscreen?

A: About every two hours, depending on your activities. Sweat, heat, and swim breaks can all contribute to diminishing the efficacy of the SPF. Read the bottle for specifics, as different sunscreens have different amounts of staying power. But be wary of any sunscreens that boast all-day protection—there's really no such thing.

Q: My skin is supersensitive. What kind of sunscreen should I use?

A: Opt for fragrance-free, broad-spectrum sunscreens with chemical-free blockers like titanium dioxide or zinc oxide.

Q: Am I at risk for skin cancer even if I don't ever burn?

A: Yes. Depending on your family history and other factors, you may still be at risk. The bottom line is that you should protect yourself when out in the sun because you just can't be sure.

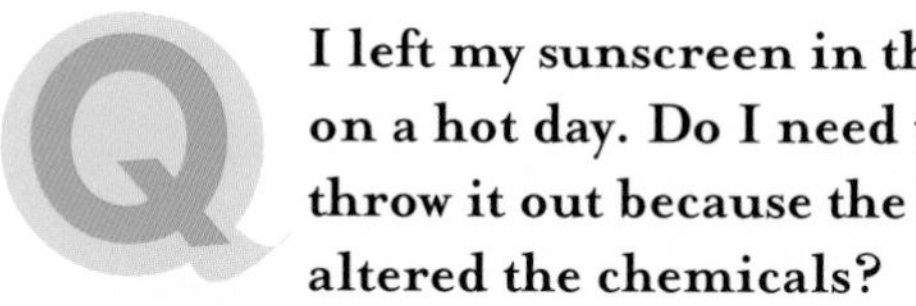

I left my sunscreen in the car on a hot day. Do I need to throw it out because the heat altered the chemicals?

A: Nope. Because the formula is designed to remain stable in the heat, you can feel good about keeping that same bottle on hand.

Does sunscreen expire?

A: Yes. Normally sunscreen is good for up to three years, but most reputable brands stamp an expiration date right onto the product. Make sure you check it out before you buy it.

Are darker skin tones safe from UV rays?

A: Not necessarily. Darker skin has more melanin, which is better at protecting against UV rays than lighter skin, making darker-skinned people at lower risk for sunburns and for skin cancer. But even though it is unusual, there are still cases of people with dark skin being diagnosed with melanoma and other skin cancers that resulted from prolonged sun exposure. Bottom line: Sun protection is necessary no matter your skin tone.

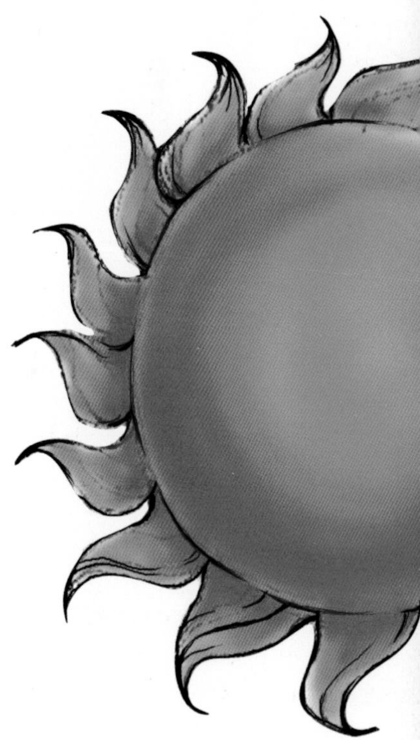

CHAPTER 7

At the Spa

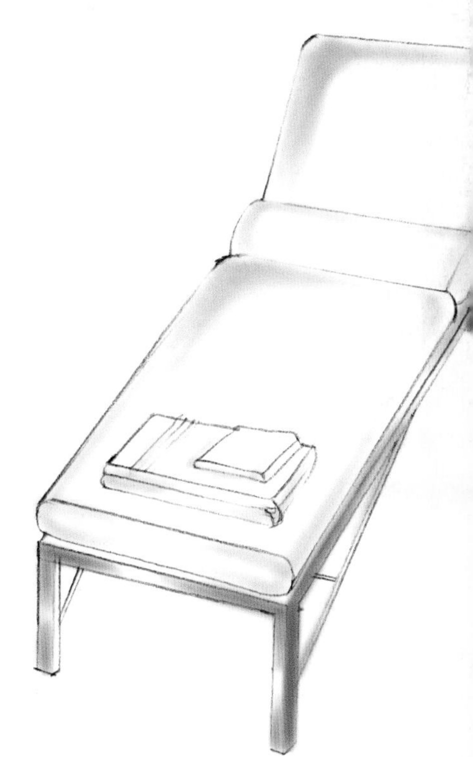

So you've found your prescription for perfect skin. Now the fun starts! Whether you splurge for a day at a spa, make regular visits to the dermatologist, or prefer to have your very own skin clinic at home, here's what you need to know.

THE SPA FACIAL

What it is:

A deep, prolonged cleansing and toning of the skin on your face.

Who it's designed for:

Anyone and everyone. Be sure to discuss your skin issues with the person administering the facial. Don't keep the fact that your skin is highly prone to acne under wraps, or you may find yourself paying for the facial in more than just the cash price.

These days, facials can be practically monogrammed for you, so feel free to customize yours to your specific needs.

How it works:

Today there are countless options—oxygen-infusing, acne-fighting, and even wrinkle-banishing. Most facials, however, involve exfoliation and then a delivery of the ingredients aimed at fixing whatever ails you. Need some glow? You'll probably get some combination of an alphahydroxy acid. Want to get rid of zits? Your facial will likely involve extractions and a dose of salicylic acid.

THE DIY FACIAL

At some fancy-pants spas, one facial can cost upward of $200! A more practical option might be to administer a facial from your own fridge. The following recipes use natural ingredients (see page 78 for the lowdown on the various ingredients and what they're good for).

Note: Always do a patch test first with a new product, especially if you have allergies or sensitive skin.

1. For glowy skin

1 avocado
1½ teaspoons olive oil

Peel and de-pit the avocado, then mash it in a small bowl with a fork. Add the olive oil and stir together. Apply to your face, wait 5 to 10 minutes, and rinse with warm water. Wash and moisturize your face as you regularly would.

2. The Moisturizing Special

1 tablespoon honey
1 egg yoke
1 teaspoon olive oil

Beat the egg yolk, then add the oil and mix well. Spoon in the honey and blend it all together. Spread it all over your face, being careful to avoid your eyes, and leave it on for 15 minutes before rinsing it off with warm water. Follow up with your regular cleanser and moisturizer.

Plan Wisely

Don't make any big plans post-facial or get it done, say, the day of your sister's wedding. Everyone reacts differently to facials, and you'll want to give your face the chance to rest for 24 hours.

3. To combat oily skin

6 slices of cucumber
1 egg white
1 tablespoon lemon juice

Blend all of the ingredients and chill them in the fridge for 10 to 15 minutes. Smear the spread on your face and relax for 15 minutes. Towel it off first and then rinse with warm water.

4. The Full-Body Exfoliator

½ cup almonds
¼ cup plain oatmeal
1 cup plain yogurt

In a food processor, chop up the almonds and the oatmeal until they are very fine (like sand granules). Stir those into the bowl of yogurt until completely mixed. Right before you take a shower, rub the mixture over any dry or scaly portions of your body and slough of dead skin. Rinse off in the shower and finish with your regular moisturizer.

CHEMICAL PEEL

What it is:

Think of a chemical peel as a facial hopped up on some serious Red Bull. Best administered by a dermatologist, a chemical peel helps improve the complexion by applying a chemical mixture (which typically includes glycolic, salicylic, or lactic acid) that forces the top layer of skin to "peel" off and make way for a smoother, more even-toned layer of skin.

Who it's designed for:

If you have mild to moderate acne, uneven skin tone, or want smoother skin, your dermatologist might start you out on a regimen of chemical peels. They're also helpful for skin discolorations, freckles, or overall blotchiness.

How it works:

After the dermatologist cleans your skin (to remove any excess oils), the peel is painted on your face and left there for about 5 minutes. A note to first-timers: You will feel a pretty noticeable hotness followed by some stinging, kind of like a minor sunburn.

MICRODERMABRASION

What it is:

An exfoliation intended to yield a smoother, more glowing complexion.

Who it's designed for:

People who have problems with blotchiness and uneven skin texture. Milder than a chemical peel, this is often an option for those with sensitive skin.

How it works:

With a buffing tool, tiny crystals of aluminum oxide are rubbed over the face in a circular motion in order to remove the top layer of skin. While the skin heals, the surface improves. This procedure is typically sold in packages of 6 to 8 sessions, all of which are necessary in order to see results.

insane in the membrane

People will do some pretty crazy things when presented with the promise of good skin—even use nightingale excrement. In fact, the Japanese have been using nightingale droppings, also known as *uguisu no fun*, as a facial cleanser for centuries. Apparently, these little bird doodles help to remove pollutants and blackheads, and produce smooth, porcelain-like skin.

nature's remedies

While it's fun to go to the spa for a day and treat yourself to top-of-the-line beauty products, it's good to remember that some of the best ingredients for your skin can be found in your own backyard (or at your local grocer).

FOOD	Apricot	Cucumber	Banana	Lemons	Honey
WHAT IT DOES	Clarifies oil, cleans deep pores	Lightens skin, cools irritated skin, reduces under-eye puffiness	Hydrates normal skin	Works as an excellent antioxidant; exfoliates skin and keeps it looking bright	Known as a natural moisturizer for its water-retaining properties
HOW TO USE IT	Pulverize the juicy part and scrub on your face	Puree the cucumber and then strain it, saving the juice to use like a toner; or slice up the cucumber and put the slices in the refrigerator	Mash the banana and mix it with yogurt; apply like a mask	Dilute fresh lemon juice with water, and use it like a toner	Add other hydrating agents (like olive oil or milk) and use the blend as a face mask or soothing bath

Of course, if you have a massive breakout, you're going to need more than a couple of apricots, but for general skin upkeep and at-home spa fun, it's good to know what various foods can do for your skin.

Oatmeal	**Yogurt**	**Egg White**	**Olive Oil**	**Avocado**
Acts as a deep cleanser and moisturizer used to exfoliate and soften skin	Works as a non-irritating soother and cleanser for body skin and scalp	The proteins in egg whites can tighten up pores (temporarily) and degrease a shiny face	Known as a heavy hydrator and antioxidant	Works as a natural emollient packed with vitamins A, D, and E
Use it as a base for a comforting soak or a rejuvenating scrub	Mix the plain variety with an exfoliating agent for a soothing slough, or use the yogurt as a post-wax salve to calm redness and comfort skin	Use it as a base for a face mask; mix in some cooling agents (like cucumbers) to give skin a healthy glow	Use it as a shaving oil, body moisturizer, and cuticle treatment	Use it as a mask to achieve hydrated, radiant skin

CHAPTER 8

The 411 on Makeup

You know how a cupcake is super delicious whether it's topped with pink icing and sprinkles or it's simply plain and sweet? You should adopt a similar perspective with makeup. You can look gorgeous with it, but equally gorgeous without it. The key thing to remember is that makeup is available to enhance your best features or disguise a little problem—it is not there to mask your beautiful face.

It's entirely possible that you're a girl who loves to play around with makeup and wear it every day, or you might prefer just a dab of concealer and some lip balm. That's the fun of makeup: You make the choice! But, as with anything, you should know what you're dealing with. Here's a deeper look at makeup's history, best uses, and effects on your skin.

A TIMELINE OF MAKEUP

Ever wonder how it became "beautiful" to have deep-red lips? Or who decided that glowy skin was "in"? Makeup has been around a lot longer than you think. Here's a timeline of how it's all played out.

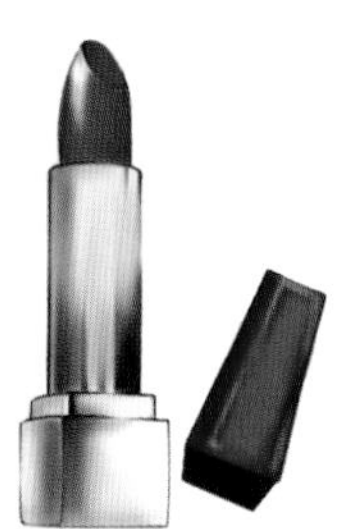

3500 BC: Records cite the first appearance of makeup in ancient Egyptian tombs, where archeologists have found pots for kohl, a naturally occurring paint used to rim eyes, as well as spoonlike makeup applicators, buried along with ancient rulers. But makeup in those days wasn't just for beauty. In fact, one type of lead (yes, lead) called galena was considered a sort of makeup, worn as eye protection under the powerful Egyptian sun (by deflecting it), as well as a deterrent against flies. Eye makeup was also believed to carry psychic protection; Egyptian mothers lined the eyes of their babies in an effort to protect them from "the evil eye."

17th Century: Perfumes and cosmetics became more mainstream in Europe, and aristocratic women powdered their faces with white makeup. (A tan was seen as a mark of the lower class, since most of the aristocrats didn't work outdoors and subsequently avoided the sun.)

19th Century: In Japan, geishas—female performing artists and consorts—wore lipstick made from crushed safflower petals and used white rice powder on their faces.

20th Century: In France—at the behest of French scientists—beauty aids began popping up all over the country. And in the United States, the Food, Drug, and Cosmetic Act of 1938 opened the floodgates for companies like Revlon, Elizabeth Arden, and Hollywood favorite Max Factor to build their own powerhouse makeup brands. Essentially, the new act protected consumers from being misled by the claims of unregulated beauty companies. (For example, prior to this act, there was a product called Lash-Lure, which was an eyelash dye that claimed to make lashes more defined. However, the formula wasn't overseen by government regulations, and it turned out to be unsafe, even blinding some women.)

TITANS OF THE BEAUTY INDUSTRY

Like Mrs. Fields has her cookies and Duncan Hines his cake mix, there are also big-time beauty product mavens who started mega enterprises that still exist today. Here are three of the most well-known.

Charles Revson

Charles Revson, founder of Revlon cosmetics, began the company in 1932 at age 25 with his brother, Joseph, and chemist Charles Lachman. They began by developing a line of nail polish, and soon turned their company into a multibillion-dollar empire, making cosmetics, perfumes, and skin care products. Throughout the years, Charles Revson developed a reputation for being a cutthroat businessman, but he was also known as a very hands-on innovator. In fact, he often tested the nail polish on his own nails, and even took phone calls from Revlon customers to hear their thoughts on his brand.

Coco Chanel

You've probably seen the famous double C logo on many celebs, but did you know that those are the initials of the woman who started the brand in 1913? French entrepreneur Gabriel Bonheur "Coco" Chanel was most known for her fashion contributions, but she also created one of the world's most iconic perfumes, Chanel No. 5—a favorite, most famously, of Marilyn Monroe's. The empire Coco Chanel has left behind creates every conceivable cosmetic and has a high-tech skin care line dedicated to keeping skin clean and radiant.

Elizabeth Arden

Perhaps motivated by her real name, Florence Nightingale Graham, this Canadian businesswoman (who later renamed herself Elizabeth Arden) turned to science to develop her beauty products. In 1915, she released her first product, Ardena Skin Tonic, and by 1930 she launched the Eight Hour Cream, which continues to be a bestseller to this day. During her career, she operated out of her iconic red-doored Manhattan salon and developed a cosmetics line, as well as a line of fragrances. Since her death in 1966, the company has stayed true to their cosmeceutical roots, using scientific research to create all their products.

HOW TO CHOOSE THE RIGHT MAKEUP FOR YOU

Selecting makeup is fun, but it can also be tricky. The idea is to enhance your already beautiful and unique skin, not to look like you are preparing to audition for the traveling circus or to radically change your natural skin tone.

We've all seen that one friend OD on the bronzer and come out looking like an Oompah Loompah. Not cute. So here are some ground rules for the tinted powders and creams you apply to your face.

1. **Not everyone needs foundation.** It's tempting to get swept up in makeup mayhem and buy everything that wily counter girl has to offer you, but remember that you don't always *need* foundation. In fact, if your skin is in good shape (even-toned, clear, and smooth), you can likely skip it.

2. **Know your options.** The endless options available in makeup these days are both a blessing and a curse. For instance, how do you know whether you should use a foundation, concealer, powder, or tinted moisturizer? It all depends on your skin type. See the chart on the next page for some guidelines

SKIN TYPE	OPT FOR
Oily	A concealer-powder combo. It evens out skin tone and sops up greasiness.
Dry	A tinted moisturizer. You get coverage plus much-needed hydration.
Normal	Concealer. A dab will do you, if all you need is a little beauty boost.
Sensitive	Less is more. If you can avoid it, you should. But if you need a little coverage, hypoallergenic formulas are the way to go.

Whichever item you feel you need, use it sparingly—your skin can't handle too much of even a good thing.

3. **Don't be shady.** When choosing foundation, always pick the shade that disappears into your skin. The days of forcing your skin to go lighter or darker are over. Owning your true skin tone no matter what shade it is, is the best beauty advice there is.

If you think you are in between shades or are trying to blend your makeup in with slightly tanned skin, you can mix two colors together to get the right skin tone.

4. **Cream vs. Powder Blush?** Blush is a powerful base layer; it can give you a rosy glow that instantly brightens up your whole face. Apply it wrong, however, and you can end up looking like a clown. Make sure you use the right one for you. Use the below chart as a guide.

SKIN TYPE	OPT FOR
Oily	Powder blush. It will absorb excess grease, and the color won't budge.
Dry	Cream or gel blushes. They'll give you a shot of moisture as well as color.
Normal	Anything goes. The options are endless!
Sensitive	Powder blush. Avoid gel and cream formulas that can irritate skin.

WHO'S WHO

Maybe your mom owns stock in Revlon, and your dad is a bigger primper than Ryan Seacrest. In that case, you probably know what's what when you walk into the beauty supply store. But if you were born to less glamorous parents, or simply prefer the au naturel life, here's a glossary to help you navigate the cosmetics aisle.

Foundation: A cosmetic base used to even out complexions and create a clean canvas upon which to apply other cosmetics. Foundation comes in liquid, cream, powder, and stick form.

Concealer: A cosmetic used to cover blemished or hyperpigmented skin. Concealer comes in cream, liquid, and stick form.

Blush: Makeup used predominantly on the cheekbones to give a rosy tint.

Bronzer: Makeup used on the face—especially in the T-zone and cheekbones to give a faux tan appearance.

Powder: Flesh-tone makeup used to make the face look less shiny.

Lipstick: A colored cosmetic for the lips—usually a waxy solid in stick form.

Lipgloss: A colored cosmetic for the lips—usually made of a shiny, slightly sticky liquid.

Eye shadow: A cosmetic applied to the eyelids, used to accent and enhance the eyes. Eyeshadows come in various colors in cream, powder, and gloss forms.

Eyeliner: A cosmetic used to emphasize the contour of the eyes above and beneath the upper and lower lash lines. Eyeliners come in gel, liquid, and pencil forms.

Mascara: A liquid cosmetic normally applied with a wand that's used to darken and thicken eyelashes.

Tinted moisturizer: A sheer, colored liquid moisturizer that offers a lighter textured alternative to foundation. It's used to even out complexions and add luster to skin tone.

BEAUTY PRODUCT BREAKDOWN

The process of buying makeup can raise a lot of questions. Is a more expensive product a better one? Does fancy packaging preserve mascara? Will cheaper eye shadows stay on as long? Here's a primer to the business of get-pretty products.

Drugstore Makeup

Aliases: Mass-brand makeup

Usual Suspects: L'Oreal, Maybelline, Wet n' Wild, Cover Girl

Loved for: The prices! The convenience! The trendiness! What could be better than finding a lip gloss in the color of the moment while you're buying a notebook, picking up an iced tea, and buying a pack of gum at your local drugstore? Only the fact that it probably costs less than $10!

Works for: All skin types. Unless your skin is of the prescription-guarded sensitive variety, mass brands offer a wide tons of choices for all skin types and tones.

Latest developments: Thanks to consumer demand, many of these companies are launching environmentally friendly products that contain minerals and use biodegradable packaging.

Masstige/Premium Makeup

Aliases: Indie-brand makeup

Usual suspects: Urban Decay, Korres, Lorac

Loved for: Middle-of-the-road prices for cool, under-the-radar products that normally have a very unique touch. The alterna-vibe appeals to your inner individualist (think: a shiny pink lip gloss called Pretty Pepto), but the product maintains a real-deal feel. And the formula might also be infused with an untapped, trendy ingredient.

Works for: All skin types. Many masstige items blend the high-tech ingredients of a prestige product with the low-maintenance production of a mass item. They're mostly found in beauty emporium stores or among the offerings of hip fashion boutiques.

Latest developments: Interesting partnerships. Because of their unfussy company frameworks, masstige brands can partner up with cool bands, unique spokespeople, and off-the-beaten-path causes.

Prestige Makeup

Aliases: High-end cosmetics

Usual suspects: Chanel, Dior, MAC

Loved for: The packaging, name, and innovation. Sure, a lip gloss by one of these designers can run you almost $30, but that's a lot less than you'd pay for a purse with the same label. Additionally, many of the ingredients are fancy and French and the product itself comes housed in deluxe packaging.

Works for: All skin types—even highly sensitive. Since they're mostly sold at department store counters or cosmetics stores, you'll get some extra help in the form of store employees. Be forewarned though: Since many of them work on a commission, don't take every recommendation they make to heart. Go in with a clear idea of what you need and what you're willing to spend.

Latest developments: Customization. No matter how complicated your skin is, prestige brands are able to accommodate. Hydrating cleanser? Check. Heavy-duty moisturizer that's also oil-free? Got that, too.

Mineral Makeup

Aliases: Natural cosmetics

Usual suspects: Bare Escentuals, Physician's Formula, Burt's Bees

Loved for: While most non-mineral makeup contains chemicals, dyes, and parabens, mineral makeup is made of things that are pure from the earth, such as mica, zinc oxide, and titanium dioxide. Generally speaking, it's also non-comedogenic (meaning it won't stuff up your pores). Also, most mineral makeup contains an SPF of at least 15, thanks in part to the inclusion of titanium dioxide and zinc oxide—but if you are out in the sun a lot, you should still probably apply sunscreen, as you don't reapply your makeup the same way you'd reapply sunscreen, and the SPF would subsequently lose some of its effectiveness.

mineral
makeup
blush
spf 15

Works for: All skin types, but particularly sensitive skin. Because some of the ingredients have anti-inflammatory properties, mineral makeup works well for sensitive skin that may experience redness. However, if you do have sensitive skin, beware of an ingredient called bismuth oxychloride. It's the stuff used to give the makeup it's shimmery appearance, but it can also be highly irritating and cause breakouts.

Latest developments: Mineral makeup had been given a bad rep for being a little less sexy than its non-mineral counterparts, but now it's showing up in all the hot, trendy shades and sleeker packaging (typically ecofriendly).

GOTCHA COVERED

No matter how good a shape your skin is in, everyone has the occasional spot or bump or mark that they'd rather keep as their little secret. Here are a few tips to keep your complexion's conundrums as covert as possible!

Zits

So you have a zit that you really want to make disappear. Here's what to do

1. Medicate the pimple with benzoyl peroxide or salicylic acid.
2. Apply your foundation (or if you don't use foundation, apply your moisturizer).
3. Using a concealer in either a cream or stick formula, in a yellow base that matches your skin tone, dab some on with your ring finger or a brush.

4. Set it with loose powder.
5. Hands off! Nothing can ruin a good hide-the-zit job like fussing with the disguise.

Dark Circles

Whether you've been studying all night for a final or just hanging out a little too late with the girls, under-eye circles can creep up on you and make you look as haggard as you feel. Fixing it, though, can wake up your face and restore that refreshed look. Try this.

1. Use a cream stick concealer or a foundation stick in a color that most closely matches your foundation and

natural skin color—if it's too light it will highlight the circles, and if it's too dark the circles will look shadowy and way darker.

2. Swab a concealer brush onto the stick and paint it on to the circles; using a brush is the only way to get good coverage without the look of wearing heavy makeup. Apply by starting at the inner corner of your eye and working your way down, underneath your lower lashes.
3. Finish up the job by patting—not rubbing—it in with your finger until it blends perfectly.
4. Get some sleep that night!

Scars

Perhaps you're fortunate enough to be out of the acne phase—lucky you! But the transition process to flawless skin could take a little time and could also mean dealing with some scarring. The good news is that most scars diminish over time, and while you're waiting, you can fake perfect skin with a little help from a trusty concealer. Here's how.

1. Using a water-based coverup (avoid oil-based if you can, as it tends to clog pores), in a shade that's about one or two shades lighter than your natural skin tone, pat a few dots over scars.
2. Add a little powder over the concealer to seal it in and create a smooth finish.

What exactly is hypoallergenic makeup?

The term *hypoallergenic* is supposed to mean that the product is safe for skin that's prone to allergic reactions. But is it really healthier? Or is it just hype? According to the United States Food and Drug Administration (FDA), it's a little bit of both. Because the US does not regulate the use of the term hypoallergenic, it's up to the companies that use the label to be on their best behavior. So even though the FDA cannot guarantee that products labeled hypoallergenic are actually safe for sensitive skin, there are many reliable companies that do clinical testing with their products to prove their efficacy.

To protect yourself against getting duped, make sure you read ingredient labels and—if your skin is highly sensitive—check in with a dermatologist before using any new items.

THE TRUTH ABOUT ORGANICS

What does organic mean? No matter how green you consider yourself or how many times you've seen *An Inconvenient Truth*, you can't deny that the recent influx of organic and natural beauty products is a tad daunting to navigate. If something is 97 percent organic, what exactly does that mean? And is a product that is "all natural" just as good as something that is "organic"? To date, there aren't any definitive answers, but there are some guidelines that can clarify what's on the shelves at your local cosmetics store.

According to the United States Department of Agriculture (USDA), which makes decisions about food labeling, organic is a word that refers to the farming, handling, and manufacturing of food. Essentially, this means that organic farms avoid pesticides, chemical fertilizers, bioengineering, and radiation (to sterilize produce). Environmentalists say that organic ingredients are richer in vitamins and nutrients, not to mention that organic products are safer because they haven't been exposed to toxic chemicals, such as pesticides, which could lead to diseases like cancer.

The same standards hold for organic makeup. For an even better idea of what you're buying, see the following rundown.

Certified Organic

According to the USDA, products bearing this label (below) must contain at least 95 percent organically grown ingredients.

100 Percent Organic Products

For a product to be given this claim, every single ingredient in the product must be organically grown (this does not include water and salt, because—under the USDA certification process—these ingredients don't qualify). You'll see the same symbol as the one above, but it will say 100 percent organic somewhere on the container.

Eco-Cert

This label signifies that at least 95 percent of the ingredients are organic. Products earn this label not through the USDA, but by an independent European agency called Eco-Cert.

Natural

The USDA does not regulate the use of the word "natural," so be careful when buying a "natural" product. After all, poison ivy is "natural," but that's not the sort of thing you want in your beauty product, right? Natural does not always mean safer. That moniker can also mean that just one ingredient in there is natural, or that the product is paraben-free, or simply that the ingredients are plant-derived. Make sure you do your research and carefully read ingredients before getting duped by a good marketing campaign that overuses the word "natural."

PARABENS

Parabens have become somewhat of a dreaded buzzword in recent years with people swearing off products that contain them and beauty companies touting new lines of cosmetics that omit them. So, what's all the fuss about?

According to the FDA, parabens are the most widely used preservatives in cosmetic products. Companies use parabens in order to protect foundations and lip glosses from any kind of microbial growth. There have been a lot of questions raised over the past five to seven years about the safety of parabens. Some reports have linked them to the estrogen-mimicking effects that can result in breast cancer. However, other studies have found that based on the small amount of parabens people are typically exposed to, it's unlikely that parabens could increase cancer risk.

So, since evidence is inconclusive, it's up to you to decide if you want to use products with parabens in them. Companies are required by law to include all ingredients—including these preservatives—on their packaging labels, so if you want to avoid them, it's easy: Look for the words methylparaben, propylparaben, butylparaben, or benzylparaben.

mix-it-yourself makeup!

On a budget? Pocket that $10 and get thee to a kitchen to cook up your own lip gloss.

Note: Always do a patch test first with a new product, especially if you have allergies or are prone to skin sensitivity.

Cranberry-Orange Lip Gloss

- 10 fresh cranberries
- 2 drops of orange oil
- 1 teaspoon sweet almond oil
- 1 teaspoon honey
- 1 drop of vitamin E oil

1. In a microwave-safe bowl, mix all of the ingredients together.
2. Microwave for 2 minutes and 30 seconds, until the mixture begins to boil. Microwave strengths vary, so you may need to add 30 seconds. If you're using a stovetop, boil the ingredients in a pot over medium-high heat.
3. With a fork, begin to crush and split the cranberries.
4. Stir the mixture until it's as smooth as you can get it.
5. Let the mixture cool down for five minutes, and run it through a strainer.
6. Mix it together again and let it cool for a few hours.
7. Once it's cool—and semi-solid—pour it into a portable container.
8. Apply and remember: It goes on your lips, not in your mouth!

QUESTIONS and Answers

Q: I've been using the same makeup for a few years without any problems, but recently my skin has broken out. Could I suddenly be allergic?

A: It's possible. It's also possible that you're not keeping your makeup applicators, like brushes or sponges, clean enough. It's a commonly overlooked issue, but one that's super important. Be sure to wash your makeup tools every three months or so, and don't share with anyone else. Wash them in warm water with a very mild cleaner, and let them dry flat. If you're still breaking out, you may want to start phasing out your products in favor of hypoallergenic ones. You may also simply be developing acne or another skin condition, in which case you should make an appointment with your dermatologist.

Q: Can using foundation or concealer make my skin break out even worse?

A: If you are breaking out into a rash from a product, you might be allergic to it. If you start noticing pimples, there's also a possibility that the formula you're using is comedogenic and is clogging your pores. Make sure you're doing everything else the same (you know, washing your face, moisturizing, the whole shebang), so that you get a good feel for whether or not the foundation is what's wreaking havoc on your skin. If you find that it is your new foundation, obviously discontinue use.

Another option: If your skin is breaking out a lot, look for a formula that contains actual zit-fighting skin helpers, like salicylic acid, benzoyl peroxide, or tea tree oil.

What's the best way to match foundation to the face?

A: Think of your foundation as a secret agent. It has a super important job but should never announce its presence—otherwise it kind of ruins the whole operation. So proper color matching is key.

First, scope out the makeup counters and test out (on your cheek, if possible) a few different shades in a formula that suits your skin. (Using your forearm is not the same; the skin there is generally lighter than on your more sun-exposed face.) The shade you choose should blend right into your skin and be barely detectable. If you can't get an exact match, err on the lighter side of the spectrum; you can balance out the tone with bronzers and blush. If you accidentally go home with a formula that's a touch too dark, you can lighten it up by mixing it with your daily moisturizer.

And don't get caught up in the shade name. One brand's "Ivory," may be another brand's "Light," whereas someone's "Mocha" could be another one's "Medium-Dark." They're just guidelines—what matters is the color inside.

beat the red

Sometimes, you can deal with hiding the size of the pimple, but it's the redness that's the dead giveaway when you're trying to conceal it. Solution? Visine! It's a well-kept Hollywood secret, but using a few dabs of the clear eyedrops can help take the red right out of that zit. Apply it first to a cotton swab and then dab it on the zit. A word of caution though: Don't do this to a particularly raw zit, as it can irritate it further.

INDEX

Lori Bergamotto

Lori Bergamotto began her career in the beauty industry as an intern and assistant at *Glamour* magazine, then went on to work as a beauty editor at *Lucky* and then as the beauty director at *Teen People*. She is currently the contributing style editor at *People StyleWatch* and a freelance writer living in New York City. Her work has appeared in *Real Simple*, *In Style*, *San Diego Magazine*, *FOAM*, *Cookie*, *Lucky*, and *Glamour*. She has been a featured beauty and style expert on TV with appearances on MTV, VH1, E!, CNN, CBS's *Early Show*, NBC's *Today Show*, and *The Tyra Banks Show*.

Acknowledgements From the Author

I would like to thank Dr. Rachel Herschenfeld, Ziki Dekel L.Ac. Angela Ene, Andrea Miller, Jennifer Allyn, and the American Academy of Dermatology for helping me tackle the complicated and fascinating subject of the skin. A huge thanks to Karen Macklin for being a remarkably patient, understanding, and genius editor, and to Hallie Warshaw, Tanya Napier, and everyone at Zest Books for all of their help and guidance. To Felicia Milewicz, for nurturing my career and my spirit from the start. Thank you to all of my fabulous friends and to the Bergamotto, Gesumaria, and Aronskind families, particularly the world's most amazing parents, Joanne and Bob Bergamotto; incredibly supportive sister and brother-in-law, Chrissy and Blake DeSimone; and remarkable grandparents, Joseph and Leslie Gesumaria, and Rose and the late Nicola Bergamotto for all of their love and unparalleled encouragement. To Nick Bergamotto, whose strides in the brave battle against melanoma continue to be an inspiration. To the Travisanos, thank you for being such a loving and welcoming surrogate family; and to the Barnhorsts, for always treating me so warmly and like one of your own. And to my biggest fan: Nicholas Barnhorst, from his biggest fan: me; thank you for being an endless source of love, humor and friendship.